THE
ORIGINAL SOURCES
OF
THE QURAN

THE ORIGINAL SOURCES OF THE QURAN.

BY THE

REV. W. ST CLAIR TISDALL,
M.A., D.D.

GYAN

Published by

GYAN

Gyan Publishing House
5, Ansari Road
Daryaganj, New Delhi-110002
Phone: 011-47034999, 9811692060
E-mail: books@gyanbooks.com

Distribution Network
gyanbooks.com
India, USA, Canada, UK, Australia

ISBN: 978-93-6208-511-5 (HB)
First Published, 1905

2nd Impression 2024

Printed at: Gyan Press, Delhi.

THE ORIGINAL SOURCES OF THE QURAN
Author: REV. W. ST CLAIR-TISDALL

THE ORIGINAL SOURCES OF THE QUR'ÂN.

THE ORIGINAL SOURCES OF THE QUR'ÂN.

BY THE

REV. W. ST. CLAIR TISDALL, M.A., D.D.

Author of "The Religion of the Crescent," "The Noble Eightfold Path," "Manual of Muhammadan Objections," &c., &c.

SOCIETY FOR PROMOTING CHRISTIAN KNOWLEDGE.

LONDON: NORTHUMBERLAND AVENUE, W.C.;

43, QUEEN VICTORIA STREET, E.C.;

BRIGHTON: 129 NORTH STREET

NEW YORK: E. S. GORHAM

1911

TO

SIR WILLIAM MUIR, K.C.S.I.

LATE PRINCIPAL OF THE UNIVERSITY OF EDINBURGH

AS

A SLIGHT TOKEN OF RESPECT AND ESTEEM.

PREFACE

THE work which is now offered to the student of Comparative Religion is the result of many years' study of various Oriental Religions ancient and modern. Except in Chapter IV, where I have made much use of Rabbi Abraham Geiger's "Was hat Mohammed aus dem Judenthume aufgenommen?" I am not to any great extent indebted to any others who have laboured in the same field. Wherever I have been conscious of any indebtedness, I have fully acknowledged it in the text or notes.

An investigation of the sources from which Islâm has sprung would be valueless, unless based upon a thorough personal study of the various ancient records quoted. This I can honestly claim to have undertaken. All the translations I give, from whatever language, are my own, except one or two passages from the Chinese, which language I have not carefully studied. The translations which I have in every other case given are as literal as possible, in some instances too literal to be elegant. But it seemed to me necessary to be *exact* in order to place the reader in a position to judge for himself of the correctness or incorrectness of my arguments. In each case I have given references to the works in which the translated passages will be found in the original languages.

I have used an exact system of transliteration for Arabic names (except in the case of the cities of Mecca and Medina), but it is one which to Arabic scholars will need no explanation.

A shorter work of mine on the same subject appeared in Persian in 1900, under the title of *Yanábí'u'l Islám*. It was very favourably reviewed[1] by that veteran scholar Sir W. Muir, to whom all students of Islâm are so much indebted for his able works on the history of Muḥammad and his successors, and has since been translated into Urdû and Arabic. Sir W. Muir has also published an English epitome of the little book. The present work is the result of further study, and has been written at the invitation of many friends, who wished to have the whole matter treated from an English standpoint, which was undesirable when I first dealt with the subject in an Eastern tongue and therefore from an Oriental point of view.

W. S. C. T.

[1] In the *Nineteenth Century* for December, 1900.

Note. The Frontispiece is not quite the same vignette as that described and explained in pp. 203–5.

TABLE OF CONTENTS

THE ORIGINAL SOURCES OF THE QUR'ÂN.

CHAPTER I.

INTRODUCTORY.

THERE is much truth in the dictum of the ancient Greek philosopher Democritus that "Nothing has sprung from nothing." Islâm, as the Religion of Muḥammad is called by its adherents, is certainly no exception to this rule. The important part which that religion has played for good or ill in the history of the human race and the widespread influence which it still continues to exert in many Eastern lands render an investigation of its origin of interest to everyone who, whether from a religious, a historical, or a merely philosophical standpoint, desires to investigate one of the most important movements in the history of the human race. The labours of such writers as Sprenger and Weil in Germany and of Sir W. Muir in England enable us to know all that need be known regarding the life and character of Muḥammad and the history of the Muḥammadan world. With these matters therefore it is unnecessary for us here to deal. It is also a matter of common knowledge that Muḥammadans profess to derive their religion directly from Muḥammad himself. They assert that he was the last and greatest of the Prophets, and that their faith rests upon the Qur'ân, which contains the Divine Revelation which he was commissioned to deliver to men. In addition to this they attach great importance to the authoritative Traditions (*Aḥâdîth*) handed down orally from the lips of their Prophet through a long series of his followers, and only in much later times committed to writing. These two, the Qur'ân and the Traditions, taken together, form the foundation of Islâm. Much importance is also attached to early commentators on the Qur'ân, and to the deductions from it made by early jurists and doctors of the law. But in our investigation of the origin of Islâmic beliefs and practices we are but little concerned with these latter, except in so far as they throw light on what is really believed by Muslims. Even the Traditions themselves play but a subordinate part in our inquiry, since their authority—from the European point of view at least—is so very uncertain. Different sects of Muḥammadans, too, accept different collections of Traditions[1]: and even the collectors

[1] Those accepted by the Sunnîs are: (1) The *Muwaṭṭá* of Mâlik ibn Ans, (2) the *Jâmi'uṣ Ṣaḥîḥ* of Bukhârî, (3) the *Ṣaḥîḥ* of Muslim, (4) the *Sunan* of Abû Dâûd Sulaimân, (5) the *Jâmi'* of Tirmidhî, and (6) the *Kitâbu's Sunan* of Muḥammad ibn Yazîd ibn Mâjah al Qazwînî. The Shî'ahs, on the other hand, accept

of these Traditions themselves confess that many of those which they record are of doubtful accuracy. As the Traditions deal for the most part, moreover, with the sayings and doings of Muḥammad, we shall have occasion to refer to them only in cases in which they amplify or explain the teaching of the Qur'ân on certain points. The latter book contains some obscure and difficult passages, the meaning of which requires to be explained by reference to Tradition. For example, the fiftieth Sûrah or chapter of the Qur'ân is entitled "Qâf," and is denoted by the Arabic letter of that name. It is not possible to be quite certain what is meant by this until we consult the Traditions, which tell us what is to be believed concerning Mount Qâf[1], to which the name of the Sûrah is held to contain a reference. Again, when in the Sûrah entitled

no traditions as authoritative except those contained in (1) the *Kâfi* of Abû Ja'far Muḥammad (A. H. 329), (2) the *Man lâ yastaḥdirahu'l Faqîh* of Shaikh 'Alî (A. H. 381), (3) the *Tahdhîb* of Shaikh Abû Ja'far Muḥammad (A. H. 466), (4) the *Istibṣâr* of the same author, and (5) the *Nahju'l Balâghah* of Sayyid Raḍî (A. H. 406). The student will find in the Introduction to the third edition of Sir W. Muir's *Life of Mahomet* an admirable investigation of the sources at our disposal for information regarding Muḥammad's life, and also an account of the way in which the Qur'ân assumed its present form, together with a discussion of the value and reliability of Tradition. It is, therefore, unnecessary to deal with the matter here as fully as it would otherwise have had to be treated. I may, however, add that what is said in the present chapter is drawn at first hand from the original authorities.

[1] Vide pp. 119, sqq.

"The Night Journey" (Sûrah XVII.), we read in the first verse the words, "Praise be unto Him who caused His servant to journey by night from the Sacred Mosque to the More Distant Mosque," we must naturally refer to Tradition to understand the meaning of the verse. We thus learn all that the 'Ulamâ of Islâm know for certain regarding the journey in question, generally styled the "Ascent" (*al Mi'râj*) of Muḥammad.

In dealing with the tenets and religious rites of Muslims, we shall make it our rule not to concern ourselves with any doctrine or practice which is not implicitly or explicitly taught or enjoined in the Qur'ân itself, or in those Traditions which are universally accepted by all Muḥammadan sects, with the partial exceptions of the Neo-Muḥammadans of India, who are not recognized as Muslims by the rest of the Muḥammadan world.

It may be well to point out the fact that, though a measure of inspiration is supposed to belong to the genuine and authoritative Traditions, yet their authority is very different from that of the Qur'ân, to which, however, they stand in the second place. This is indicated by the difference in the manner of speaking of these different forms of revelation. The Qur'ân is styled "Recited Revelation," and the Traditions "Unrecited Revelation," because the Qur'ân and it alone is considered to constitute the very utterance of God Himself. Hence the rule has been laid down that any Tradition, however well authenticated it may be, that is clearly contrary to a single verse of the Qur'ân must be rejected. This rule is an important one for us to observe in dealing with matters of Muḥammadan belief. It renders it unnecessary for us to involve ourselves in the mazes of the labyrinth of the controversy as to which traditions are genuine, which doubtful, and which unreliable. It is sufficient for our present purpose to note that in their written form Traditions are considerably later in date than the text of the Qur'ân.

Regarding the history of the latter, accepted as it is by all Muslims everywhere, we have fairly full and satisfactory information. Some of the Sûrahs may have been written down on any materials that came to hand by some of Muḥammad's amanuenses, of which we are told he had a considerable number, as soon as they were first recited by him. The knowledge of writing was not uncommon in his time among the Meccans, for we are informed that some of the latter, when taken captive, obtained their liberty by instructing certain of the people of Medina in the art. Whether written down at once or not, they were instantly committed to memory, and were recited at the time of public worship and on other occasions During Muḥammad's lifetime frequent reference was made to him when any doubt arose with regard to the proper wording of a passage. Tradition mentions certain Sûrahs or verses which were preserved in a written form in the houses of Muḥammad's wives during his life, and we are even told that some verses thus written were lost and never recovered. From time to time the Prophet directed newly revealed verses to be inserted in certain Sûrahs, which must therefore have already assumed form and have even received the names which they still retain. There seems, however, to have been no fixed order prescribed in which these Sûrahs should be arranged. Each formed a more or less independent whole. The task of learning the Sûrahs by heart was not only a labour of love to Muḥammad's devoted followers, but it also became a source of dignity and profit, since not only were those who could recite the largest number of verses entitled in very early times to assume the position of *Imâm* or leader in public worship, but they were also considered to have a claim to a larger share of the spoil than were other Muslims.

About a year after Muḥammad's death, as we learn from Bukhârî, the Qur'ân was first put together in a collected whole. This was done by Zaid ibn Thâbit, one of Muḥammad's friends and amanuenses, at the command of Abû Bakr. The reason for this step was that 'Umar bnu'l Khaṭṭâb, perceiving that many of the reciters of the Qur'ân had fallen in the fatal battle of Yamâmah (A. H. 12), saw reason to fear lest the Revelation should thus in whole or in part be lost. He therefore strongly urged the Khalîfah[1] to give orders that the scattered Sûrahs should be collected together and preserved in an authoritative written form. Zaid at first felt great reluctance to do what the Prophet himself had not thought fit to do, but he at last yielded to the command of the Khalîfah. The story[2] as told in his own words runs thus: "Abû Bakr said to me, 'Thou art a learned young man: we do not distrust thee: and thou wast wont to write out the Divine Revelation for the Apostle of God. Seek out the Qur'ân therefore and collect it.' If they had imposed upon me the duty of removing a mountain, it would not have weighed more heavily upon me than what he commanded me to do in the way of collecting the Qur'ân. . . . Abû Bakr did not desist from urging me to collect it, until God enlightened my breast to perceive what 'Umar and Abû Bakr's own breast had made clear to the latter. Accordingly I searched out the whole of the Qur'ân from leafless palm-branches and from white stones and from the breasts of men, until I found the conclusion of Sûratu't Taubah (Sûrah IX., v. 129) with Abû Khuzaimah the Anṣârî. I found it not with anyone else."

From the phrase "to *collect* the Qur'ân," it is evident that the book had not previously been

[1] This word is generally, but wrongly, spelt *Caliph.* It is applied to Muḥammad's successors, and means "*Vicegerent* (of the Apostle of God)."

[2] *Mishkâtu'l Maṣâbiḥ*, pp. 185 sqq., from Bukhârî.

formed into one united whole. His reverence for his master would naturally prevent Zaid from either adding to or omitting anything from the Sûrahs which were recited to him by many persons from memory, and in some cases found in writing upon the various writing materials which were then in use. The fact that certain circumstances most derogatory to Muḥammad's claim to be a Divinely commissioned prophet are still to be found in the Qur'ân is a conclusive proof of the scrupulous accuracy with which Zaid discharged the task entrusted to him. Nor would it have been possible at that time to have in any way tampered with the text. Within a year or two he had completed the work and had written down all the Sûrahs, each apparently on a separate sheet. It seems that there is some reason to believe that the present arrangement of the Sûrahs dates from that time. On what system it rests it is hard to say, except that the Sûratu'l Fâtiḥah was placed first as a sort of introduction to the book, partly no doubt because it was even then universally used as a prayer, and so was better known than any other. The other Sûrahs were arranged on the principle of putting the longest first. Thus the shortest come at the end of the book. This is almost the direct converse of their chronological order. Tradition enables us to know in what order and on what occasion most of the Sûrahs, and in certain cases some of their verses, were "revealed," but in our present inquiry it is not necessary to deal with this matter[1] at all fully, important as it doubtless is for the study of the steady development of the Faith, as it gradually took shape in Muḥammad's own mind.

Zaid on the conclusion of his work handed over the manuscript, written doubtless in the so-called Cufic character, to Abû Bakr. The latter preserved it carefully until his death, when it was committed to the custody of 'Umar, after whose decease it passed into the charge of Ḥafṣah, his daughter, one of Muḥammad's widows. Copies of separate Sûrahs were afterwards made either from this or from the original authorities which Zaid had used.

Errors, or at least variations, gradually crept into the text of the Qur'ân as it was recited, and possibly also into these fragmentary copies. Abû Bakr does not seem to have caused authoritative transcripts of the single manuscript which Zaid had written to be made, and hence it could not counteract the very natural tendency to alteration, mostly or wholly unintentional, to which the Qur'ân, like every other work handed down orally, was liable. There were different dialects of Arabic then in use, and there must have been a tendency in the first

[1] The Sûrahs are arranged as nearly as possible in chronological order in Rodwell's translation of the Qur'ân, though doubtless certain early Sûrahs had verses of later date inserted into them long after they were written. See Canon Sell's "Historical Development of the Qur'ân."

place to explain certain words, and in the second to permit these dialectic paraphrases to find an entrance into the recited verses. This caused no little confusion and perplexity in the minds of pious Muslims. At last 'Uthmân, when engaged in the task of conquering Armenia and Âẕarbâîjân, was warned by Ḥudhaifah ibnu'l Yamân of the danger which there was lest the original should be very seriously corrupted in this way. Bukhârî[1] tells us that Ḥudhaifah said to 'Uthmân, "O Commander of the Faithful, restrain this people, before they differ among themselves about the Book as much as the Jews and the Christians do." The Khalîfah therefore sent to bid Ḥafṣah forward to him the original manuscript to be copied, promising to return it to her when this had been done. He then commissioned Zaid, in conjunction with three members of Muḥammad's own tribe, the Quraish, to produce a recension of the work. At least this is what his language seems to imply, for he said to the three Quraishites, "Whenever ye differ, ye and Zaid ibn Thâbit, in reference to any part of the Qur'ân, then write it in the dialect of the Quraish, for it was revealed in their language." We are told that the new recension was copied from the original manuscript, and so doubtless it was for the most part. Yet the words we have quoted prove that certain alterations must have been made, though no doubt in good faith, and prin-

[1] *Mishkâtu'l Maṣâbîḥ*, pp. 185, 186

cipally to preserve the purity of the Meccan dialect of the book. Another proof that some change was made is afforded by the statement that on this occasion Zaid recollected a verse which was not in the first copy, and which he had himself heard Muḥammad recite. He did not, however, venture to insert it merely on his own authority, but searched until he found another man who could recite it from memory. When this was done, the verse was entered in Sûratu'l Aḥzâb. Then "'Uthmân[1] returned the sheets to Ḥafṣah, and sent to every region an exemplar of what they had copied out, and with reference to every sheet and volume of the Qur'ân besides this he commanded that it should be burned."

This last proceeding may seem to us arbitrary[2], but it has succeeded in preserving the text of the Qur'ân from that day to this in practically one and the same form in all Muḥammadan lands. Even Ḥafṣah's copy, the only one which in any important respect differed from the revised edition after the execution of 'Uthmân's command, was on that account burned in Marwân's time. The *very* few differences of reading which diligent search has

[1] ردّ عثمان الصّحف الى حفصة وارسل الى كلّ افق بمُصحف ممّا نسخوا وامر بما سواه من القرآن فى كلّ صحيفة ومصحف ان يُحْرَق.

[2] See the objections stated in Al Kindi's *Apology*, Sir W. Muir's translation, pp. 72–8.

revealed in various copies of the Qur'ân now extant consist almost wholly in the position of the dots which distinguish from one another[1] the letters ت, ي and ن, and these letters have no such diacritical marks in the old Cufic alphabet.

We are therefore led to the conclusion that we still have the Qur'ân as Muḥammad left it, and hence we may, with almost perfect certainty as to the correctness of the text, proceed to study the book in order to ascertain what he taught and whence he derived the various statements and doctrines which, contained in the Qur'ân and explained and amplified in the Traditions, constitute the Religion of Islâm.

In discussing the origin of Islâm it is right in the first place to consider the statements on the subject which are made by the leading teachers and Doctors of the Law among the Muslims, and to inquire whether their opinions on this point are supported by the assertions of the Qur'ân itself. We shall then proceed to investigate the question whether it is possible for us to accept these statements as the correct explanation of the facts of the case.

It is well known that the 'Ulamâ of Islâm assert and have always asserted that the Qur'ân is the Word of God Himself, which the Most High caused to be inscribed upon "the Preserved Tablet"

[1] A few examples of such various readings occur in Sûrah VI., Al An'âm, 91.

in Heaven, long ages before the creation of the world. Although in the reign of the Khalîfah Al Ma'mûn (A.H. 198–218 = A.D. 813–33) and afterwards there occurred many fierce disputes between those who held that the Qur'ân was *eternal* and those who believed that it was *created*, into which discussion it is not necessary for us to enter, yet all Muslims have always agreed in holding that the book is not the composition of Muḥammad or of any other human author. On the contrary, they believe that it is entirely the work of God Himself, and that Muḥammad was merely His messenger in this respect, whose duty it was to receive the Divine book and communicate it to men. Tradition tells us that the book was brought down on one particular night[1] from the highest to the lowest heaven by the Archangel Gabriel, who afterwards gradually conveyed the verses and chapters to the mind and tongue of Muḥammad. Accordingly there is nothing whatever that is human about the Qur'ân: it is wholly and entirely of Divine origin.

That our readers may perceive that this is really the orthodox Muḥammadan view of the matter, we here quote two passages on the subject from the well-known Arabic writer Ibn Khaldûn. "Know therefore," he says[2], "that the Qur'ân

[1] Called the "Night of Power."

[2] فاعلم ان القرآن نزل بلغة العرب وعلى اساليب بلاغتهم وكانوا كلّهم يفهمونه ويعلمون معانيه فى مفرداته وتراكيبه وكان ينزل جملاً

descended in the language of the Arabs and in accordance with their style of eloquence, and all of them understood it and knew its various meanings in its several parts and in their relation to one another. And it continued to descend, section by section and in groups of verses, in order to explain the doctrine of the Unity of God and religious obligations, according as circumstances required. Some of these verses consist of articles of faith, and some of them of commandments for the regulation of conduct." In another passage the same writer says, "All this[1] is a proof to thee that, amid the Divine Books, it was verily the Qur'ân with which our Prophet (may God's blessings and His peace be upon him!) was inspired, in the form of something recited just as it is in its words and in its sections; whereas the Law and the Gospel on the other hand, and all the other Heavenly Books, were revealed to the Prophets in

جملاً وآيات آيات لبيان التّوحيد والفروض الدّينيّة بحسب الوقائع ومنها ما هو فى العقايد الايمانيّة ومنها ما هو فى احكام الجوارح

(Arabic Text, vol. ii., p. 391.)

[1] ويدلّك هذا كلّه على ان القران من بين الكتب الالهيّة انّما تلقاه نبيّنا صلوات الله وسلامه عليه متلوًا كما هو بكلماته وتراكيبه بخلاف التّوراة والانجيل وغيرهما من الكتب السّماويّة فأنّ الانبياء يتلقونها فى حال الوحى معانى ويعبرون عنها بعد رجوعهم الى الحالة البشريّة بكلامهم المعتاد لهم ولذلك لم يكن فيها اعجاز

(Vol. i., pp. 171, 172.)

the form of ideas when they were in a state of ecstasy, and they explained them, after their return to man's ordinary condition, in their own customary language: and therefore there is nothing miraculous in them." That is to say, the 'Ulamà of Islâm, while acknowledging that other prophets came before Muḥammad and brought Divine messages to man, yet hold that the inspiration of the Qur'ân differs not only in degree but in kind from that to which other sacred books, as for instance the Law and the Gospel, are due. The writers of these books received certain *ideas* from God in some way, but the language which they afterwards used to express these conceptions was their own, and cannot therefore claim any origin higher than the human. Muḥammad, on the contrary, heard Gabriel reading aloud or reciting in a voice distinctly audible to him every single word of the Qur'ân, according as it was inscribed on the "Preserved Tablet" in heaven. Arabic is held to be the language of heaven and of the angels, and hence in the Qur'ân we have the very words, as well as the Word, of God Himself. Words, metaphors, reflections, narratives, style, all are wholly and entirely of Divine origin.

There can be no doubt that this view is in complete accordance with the statements of the Qur'ân itself. The Divine original is styled "the Mother of the Book" (Sûrah XIII., Ar Ra'd, 39). Again and again in varied forms are such assertions as the following to be found in the Qur'ân: "Nay, it is a glorious Qur'ân in a Preserved Tablet" (Sûrah LXXXV., Al Burûj, 21, 22). The word *Qur'ân* itself denotes this, meaning "that which is *recited*." In another place we read that God Most High commanded Muḥammad to say, "God is witness between me and you, and this Qur'ân was given me by inspiration that I might warn you therewith" (Sûrah VI., Al An'âm, 19). So also in Sûrah XCVII., Al Qadr, 1, God is represented as saying with reference to the Qur'ân, "Verily We caused it to descend on the Night of Power." Such quotations might be almost indefinitely multiplied [1].

The Muḥammadan explanation of the origin of Islâm therefore, based as it ultimately is upon the Qur'ân, is that the sole Source and Fountain-head of the Religion of Islâm is God Himself. It had accordingly no human source, and no single part of it was derived directly or indirectly from earlier revelations or from other religions, though it was revealed to confirm the Law and the Gospel, and claims to agree with their original and uncorrupted teaching (cf. Sûrah LVII., Al Ḥadîd, 26, sqq.).

European readers hardly require proof that such an opinion of the origin of Islâm in general and of the Qur'ân in particular is untenable. Those who cannot read the book in the original Arabic are enabled to examine its teaching by consulting the

[1] Cf. Sûrahs IV., 84; XVII., 107; XLVI., 7; LIII., 4; &c., &c.

various translations of the Qur'ân which have been made into various European languages, the best-known of the English versions being those by Sale, Rodwell, and Palmer. To an intelligent mind the assertion which we are considering refutes itself. Moreover, the morality of the Qur'ân, its view of the Divine Nature, its anachronisms, and its many defects make it impossible for us to doubt that it is Muḥammad's own composition. When the Sûrahs are arranged in the chronological order of their composition and compared with the events in Muḥammad's life, we see that there is much truth in the statement that the passages were—not, as Muslims say, *revealed*, but—composed from time to time, as occasion required, to sanction each new departure made by Muḥammad[1]. The Qur'ân is a faithful mirror of the life and character of its author. It breathes the air of the desert, it enables us to hear the battle-cries of the Prophet's followers as they rushed to the onset, it reveals the working of Muḥammad's own mind, and shows the gradual declension of his character as he passed from the earnest and sincere though visionary enthusiast into the conscious impostor and open sensualist. All this is clear to every unprejudiced reader of the book.

At the same time the question presents itself, Whence did Muḥammad borrow the ideas, the narratives, the precepts, which he has incorporated

[1] Vide pp. 275 sqq.

into the religion which he founded? Which of these were his own invention, which of them were derived from earlier systems? To what extent had he the means of learning the teachings of those who professed other religions than his own? If he borrowed from other systems, what particular parts of the Qur'ân, what religious rites, what conceptions and narratives, what injunctions can be traced to each such source? How much of the result is due to the character of Muḥammad himself and to the circumstances of his time? Such are some of the problems which it is our object in this book to solve as clearly and as succinctly as we may. From whatever point of view we may regard the inquiry, it can hardly fail to be interesting. Such an investigation, if honestly pursued, will enable a Muslim to appreciate his ancestral faith at its real and proper value. The student of Comparative Religion will learn from such an analysis how one Ethnic Faith arose in recent historical times, though, if he is wise, he will not be led to formulate rash conclusions from a single instance. The Christian Missionary may also find it important to follow out our investigations, in order to discover in them a new method of leading Muslim inquirers to perceive the untenable nature of their position. Setting aside, however, all such considerations, we proceed to inquire what the Original Sources of the Qur'ân really were.

CHAPTER II.

THE INFLUENCE OF ANCIENT ARABIAN BELIEFS AND PRACTICES.

IN order to be able to understand the gradual development of Islâm in Muḥammad's mind, and to discover from what sources he borrowed, it is necessary in the first place to consider the religious opinions and observances of the Arabs among whom he was born and bred.

The inhabitants of Arabia were not all of one race. Arabic writers in general divide them into pure or original Arabs and those who, coming from other countries, had become Arabicized. Ḥimyarites and certain other tribes present us with traces of affinity with the Æthiopians, and the accounts which the cuneiform tablets give us of early conquests of parts of the country by the Sumerian kings of Babylonia, coupled with the fact that the early Egyptian kings for a time held sway over the Sinaitic Peninsula and possibly over other districts in the North and West, leave no doubt that there were even in early times Hamitic and other foreign elements in the population. In the days of the great Cushite monarchies in Babylonia, not only must the people of Arabia have been to some degree affected by their civilization, their trade and their ideas in general, but the influence of the religion also of these foreign nations must have been considerable. Early Arabian inscriptions prove this, containing as they do the names of such deities as Sin (the Moon-god) and 'Aththar (Ashtoreth, Ishtar), worshipped by the Sumerians in the first place and afterwards by the Semites of Babylonia, Assyria, Syria, and of some parts of Arabia. Yet, though there was doubtless a Hamitic element in the population, the great mass of the people from very early times has always been Semitic in origin, and also in language, character, and religion.

Ibn Hishâm, Ṭabarî, and other Arabian historians have preserved ancient traditions of certain Arab tribes, particularly those of the northern and western parts of the country. These agree with the statements of the Pentateuch, and give every reason to believe that most of these tribes could trace their descent to Joktan (Ar. Qaḥṭân[1]), or to Ishmael, or to Abraham's children by Keturah. Even those who had no real right to claim such lineage did so in Muḥammad's time. The Quraish, his own tribe, claimed descent from Abraham through Ishmael. Although it may be considered

[1] It is unnecessary for us to discuss the anachronism involved in this identification.

impossible to prove this, the very fact that such was the belief of the tribe would naturally enlist a certain amount of popular sympathy in Muḥammad's cause, when he claimed to be commissioned to recall his people to the "faith of Abraham," whom they boasted of as their ancestor.

There seems good reason to believe that the original religion of the children of Shem was the worship of the One[1] God. Although polytheism had even in very early times found an entrance into Arabia, in part doubtless through the foreign influences already referred to, yet the belief in the One true God had never entirely faded away from the minds of the people. The most binding agreements between different tribes were confirmed by an oath taken in calling on the name of God (*Allâh, Allâhumma*), and the expression, "An enemy of God," was deemed the most opprobrious that could be used. It is possible that we may see in the Book of Job the proof that even in that early period the worship of the Host of Heaven was finding an entrance into the country (Job xxxi. 26–8). Herodotus (Book III., cap. 8) informs us that two deities, a male and a female, were worshipped by the Arabs in his time, and these he identifies with Dionysos and Ourania. He informs us that their names in Arabic were 'Ὀροτάλ

[1] This is not the place to enter upon the proof of the matter, but I hold that the fact stated in the text is correct, in spite of all that has recently been written on the other side.

and Ἀλιλάτ respectively. The latter is very possibly the *Allâtu* of Babylonia, and is certainly the *Al-lât* mentioned in the Qur'ân [1]. The latter word was taken to be the feminine of *Allâh* (ألله), "God:" *Allâh* itself is known to be a contraction of *Al Ilâh*, which is the word used in all the Semitic languages (in slightly varied forms) for *God*, with the definite article prefixed, so that Allâh is the exact equivalent of the Greek ὁ Θεός. The form Ἀλιλάτ which is given us by Herodotus is the uncontracted form of the feminine of the same word [2]. It is possible that the Arabs of whom Herodotus speaks [3] provided their *one* God with a female consort, after the manner of the Semites of Babylonia, who had learnt from the

[1] Sûrah LIII., 19.

[2] In Assyrian *Îlu* is God, *îlatu* is "goddess." *Allâtu* is probably from the Accadian.

[3] As we shall have to refer to it again, it may be well to quote the passage at length. It runs thus: Σέβονται δὲ Ἀράβιοι πίστις ἀνθρώπων ὁμοῖα τοῖσι μάλιστα. ποιεῦνται δὲ αὐτὰς τρόπῳ τοιῷδε· τῶν βουλομένων τὰ πιστὰ ποιέεσθαι, ἄλλος ἀνὴρ ἀμφοτέρων αὐτῶν ἐν μέσῳ ἑστεὼς λίθῳ ὀξέϊ τὸ ἔσω τῶν χειρῶν παρὰ τοὺς δακτύλους τοὺς μεγάλους ἐπιτάμνει τῶν ποιευμένων τὰς πίστις· καὶ ἔπειτα λαβὼν ἐκ τοῦ ἱματίου ἑκατέρου κροκύδα ἀλείφει τῷ αἵματι ἐν μέσῳ κειμένους λίθους ἑπτά· τοῦτο δὲ ποιέων ἐπικαλέει τόν τε Διόνυσον καὶ τὴν Οὐρανίην. ἐπιτελέσαντος δὲ τούτου ταῦτα, ὁ τὰς πίστις ποιησάμενος τοῖσι φίλοισι παρεγγυᾷ τὸν ξεῖνον, ἢ καὶ τὸν ἀστόν, ἢν πρὸς ἀστὸν ποιέηται· οἱ δὲ φίλοι καὶ αὐτοὶ τὰς πίστις δικαιεῦσι σέβεσθαι. Διόνυσον δὲ θεὸν μοῦνον καὶ τὴν Οὐρανίην ἡγεῦνται εἶναι· καὶ τῶν τριχῶν τὴν κουρὴν κείρεσθαί φασι, καθάπερ αὐτὸν τὸν Διόνυσον κεκάρθαι· κείρονται δὲ περιτρόχαλα, περιξυροῦντες τοὺς κροτάφους. οὐνομάζουσι δὲ τὸν μὲν Διόνυσον, Ὀροτάλ· τὴν δὲ Οὐρανίην, Ἀλιλάτ (Herod. Lib. III., 8).

Sumerians the idea that each deity must have his feminine[1] counterpart, just as we find among the Hindûs. On the other hand, we are not justified in believing that this was the case among all the Arabs. Certainly it was not so in Muḥammad's time, for neither the Qur'ân nor any of the remains of the most ancient poetry of the Arabs afford any trace of such a tenet. Allâh was regarded as standing alone and unapproachable, and the inferior deities peculiar to the various tribes were worshipped as intercessors with Him. These were numerous, the most important of them being Wudd, Ya'ûq, Hubal, Al-lât, 'Uzza,' and Manâh. The three latter were goddesses, and the Qur'ân reproves[2] the Arabs for styling them "daughters of God." The Arabs of that time, if we may judge from their poetry, were not very religious, but what worship they offered was mostly to these inferior deities, though doubtless regarded as through them addressed to Allâh Himself. The latter was often styled Allâh Ta'âla' (الله تعالى), or "God Most High," and this title of His was doubtless very ancient[3].

[1] Others, e.g. Prof. Sayce (in his *Lectures on the Religions of Egypt and Babylonia*), hold that this was an original Semitic idea.

[2] Sûrahs XVI., 59; LIII., 19-21, 28.

[3] The 'Οροτάλ of Herodotus has doubtless preserved in its last syllable the word *Ta'âla'*. The first part of the word is of uncertain derivation: it *may* be a corruption of *Allâh*. With *Allâh Ta'âla'* cf. the אֵל עֶלְיוֹן of Gen. xiv. 18, 19, 22.

It is not possible to suppose that the recognition of the Unity of God was introduced among the Arabs for the first time by Muḥammad. For the word *Allâh*, containing as it does the definite article, is a proof that those who used it were in some degree conscious of the Divine Unity. Now Muḥammad did not invent the word, but, as we have said, found it already in use among his fellow countrymen at the time when he first claimed to be a Prophet, a Divinely commissioned messenger. Proof of this is not far to seek. Muḥammad's own father, who died before his son's birth, was called *ʿAbdu'llâh*, "Servant of Allâh [1]." The Kaʿbah or Temple at Mecca seems long before Muḥammad's time to have been called *Baitu'llâh* or "House of Allâh." Arabic tradition asserts that a shrine for the worship of God was built on that very site by Abraham and his son Ishmael. Although we cannot regard this statement as in any sense historical, yet the tradition serves at least to show the antiquity of the worship there offered, since its origin was lost in fable. The Kaʿbah is, in all probability, the spot referred to by Diodorus Siculus [2] (B.C. 60) as containing a shrine or temple which was very specially honoured by all the Arabs. In the poems entitled Al Muʿallaqât, handed down to us from pre-Islâmic times, the

[1] So also a nephew of Muḥammad was called *ʿUbaidu'llâh*.

[2] *Ἱερὸν ἁγιώτατον ἵδρυται τιμώμενον ὑπὸ πάντων Ἀράβων περιττότερον* (Diod. Sic., Lib. III.).

word Allâh (= ὁ Θεός) is of frequent occurrence[1]. And Ibn Isḥâq, the earliest biographer of Muḥammad of whose work any certain remains have come down to us, is quoted by Ibn Hishâm as stating that the tribes of Kinânah and Quraish, when performing the religious ceremony known as the *Ihlâl*, used to address the Deity in such words[2] as these: "Labbaika, Allâhumma!—We are present in Thy service, O God; we are present in Thy service! Thou hast no partner, except the partner

[1] For example, we find in the *Dîwân* of An Nâbighah the following lines:—

لَهُمْ شِيمَةٌ لَمْ يُعْطِهَا ٱللَّهُ غَيْرَهُمْ   مِنَ ٱلْجُودِ وَٱلْأَحْلَامِ غَيْرُ عَوَازِبِ
مَحَلَّتُهُمْ ذَاتُ ٱلْإِلٰهِ وَدِينُهُمْ   قَوِيمٌ فَمَا يَرْجُونَ غَيْرَ ٱلْعَوَاقِبِ

(Poem I., ll. 23, 24, ed. Ahlwardt.)

And again:—

أَلَمْ تَرَ أَنَّ ٱللَّهَ أَعْطَاكَ سُورَةً   تَرَى كُلَّ مَلْكٍ دُونَهَا يَتَذَبْذَبُ
بِأَنَّكَ شَمْسٌ وَٱلْمُلُوكُ كَوَاكِبٌ   إِذَا طَلَعَتْ لَمْ يَبْدُ مِنْهُنَّ كَوْكَبُ

(Poem III., ll. 9, 10.)

And so also in Poem VIII., ll. 5, 6:—

وَنَحْنُ لَدَيْهِ نَسْأَلُ ٱللَّهَ خُلْدَهُ   يَرُدُّ لَنَا مُلْكاً وَلِلْأَرْضِ عَامِرَا
وَنَحْنُ نُرَجِّي ٱلْخُلْدَ إِنْ فَازَ قِدْحُنَا   وَنَرْهَبُ قِدْحَ ٱلْمَوْتِ إِنْ جَآءَ قَاهِرَا

Labîd has also the following verse:—

لَعَمْرُكَ مَا تَدْرِي ٱلضَّوَارِبُ بِٱلْحَصَى   وَلَا زَاجِرَاتُ ٱلطَّيْرِ مَا ٱللَّهُ صَانِعُ

[2] Quoted in Ibn Hishâm's *Sîratu'r Rasûl*, Egyptian edition, Part I., pp. 27, 28.

of Thy dread; Thou ownest him and whatsoever he owneth." Ibn Isḥâq rightly says that by this address they declared their belief in the unity of Allâh. He does not explain what was meant by the phrase "The partner of Thy dread:" but it may be conjectured that the reference was to some inferior deity belonging to one or other of the tribes which he mentions. But in any case the language employed shows clearly that the being referred to was not in any way placed upon an equality with Allâh. The religion of the ancient Arabs may therefore be justly compared with the Saint-worship of the Greek and Roman Churches, alike of Muḥammad's time and of our own, and with that which, in spite of the Qur'ân, is even now prevalent among Muslims. But the worship offered in such cases to saints or inferior deities is not supposed to constitute a denial of the Unity and supremacy of God, since the latter are adored only as mediators between God and man. What Ash Shahristânî tells us of the religious ideas and practices of the pre-Islâmic period in Arabia fully confirms this[1]. He divides the in-

[1] Ash Shahristânî in الملل والنّحل, quoted by Abû'l Fidâ (*Hist. Ante-Islamica*):—

والعرب الجاهليّة اصناف فصنف انكروا الخالق والبعث وقالوا بالطّبع المحيى والدّهر المفنى كما اخبر عنهم التّنزيل وَقَالُوا مَا هِيَ إِلَّا حَيَاتُنَا الدُّنْيَا نَمُوتُ وَنَحْيَا ـ وقوله[a] ـ وَمَا يُهْلِكُنَا إِلَّا الدَّهْرُ ـ

[a] Sûrah جاثيّة (Sûrah XLV., 23).

habitants of Arabia into various sects or parties, differing very much in their religious opinions. Some of them, he says, denied the existence of a Creator, the sending of prophets, and the final judgment, asserting that Nature itself was the giver of life and that Time was the universal destroyer. Others again believed in a Creator, but denied that He had ever revealed Himself by sending messengers commissioned to declare His

وصنف اعترفوا بالخالق وانكروا البعث وهم الذين اخبر الله عنهم
بقوله تعالى[b] — أَفَعَيِينَا بِالْخَلْقِ الْأَوَّلِ بَلْ هُمْ فِي لَبْسٍ مِنْ خَلْقٍ
جَدِيدٍ — وصنف عبدوا الاصنام وكانت اصنامهم مختصّة بالقبايل
فكان وُدٌّ لكلب وهو بدومة الجندل و سُوَاعٌ لهذيل ويغوث لمَذْحِج
ولقبايل من اليمن ونَسْرٌ لذى الكلاع بارض حمير ويَعُوقُ لهمذان
واللّات لثقيف بالطّايف والعُزّى لقريش وبنى كنانة ومَنَاةُ للاوس
والخزرج وهُبَلُ اعظم اصنامهم وكان هُبَلُ على ظهر الكعبة وكان
اساف ونايلى على الصّفا والمروة وكان منهم مَن يميل الى اليهود
ومنهم مَن يميل الى النّصرانيّة ومنهم مَن يميل الى الصّابيّة ويعْتقد
فى انواء المنازل اعتقاد المنجّمين فى السّيارات حتّى لا يتحرّك الّا
بنوء من الانواء ويقول مطرنا بنوء كذا وكان منهم من يعبد الملائكة
ومنهم من يعبد الجنّ وكانت علومهم علم الانساب والانواء
والتّواريخ وتعبير الرّؤيا وكان لابى بكر الصّدّيق رضى الله عنهُ فيها
يد طولى

(Fleischer's ed., pp. 178–81.) See also on the same subject Krehl, *Über die Religion der vorislamischen Araber*, pp. 4 sqq.

[b] Sûrah ق (Sûrah L., 14).

will. Others, again, worshipped idols, of which each tribe had its own. For example, the tribe of Kalb worshipped Wudd and Suwâ‘, that of Madhḥaj honoured Yaghûth, as did some of the Yamanites. The Dhû'lkilâ‘ in Ḥimyar worshipped Nasr, the Hamdhân tribe adored Ya‘ûq, that of Thaqîf in Ṭâif served Al-lât, while Al-‘Uzza' was the tutelary goddess of the Banû Kinânah and of the Quraish. The tribes of Aûs and Khazraj worshipped Manâh, and regarded Hubal as the chief of their deities. His image was placed in a most conspicuous place on the roof of the Ka‘bah. Other deities were Asâf and Nâila'. Some of the tribes had come under the influence of Jewish colonies settled near them, and accepted more or less of the teaching of the latter people. Others had become Christians, while their neighbours were inclined to accept that faith. Others, again, were under the influence of the Ṣâbians, and used to practise astrology and receive omens taken from the movements of the heavenly bodies as their guides in all actions of importance. Some worshipped angels, some the *Jinns* or evil spirits. Abû Bakr himself, who afterwards became the first Khalîfah or "Vicegerent of the Apostle of God," was at one time distinguished for his proficiency in the art of interpreting dreams.

A story [1] related by many Arabic writers, includ-

[1] In the *Mawâhibu'l luduniyyah* the tale is told in several forms. One runs thus :—

ing some of the best-known commentators on the Qur'ân, shows how readily the Arabs in Muḥam-

قدم نفر من مهاجرة الحبشة حين قراء عليه السّلام – وَالنّجْمِ إذا هَوىٰ – حتّىٰ بلغ – أفرأيتم اللات والعزّى ومناة الثالثة الأخرى – القى الشّيطان فى منيتِهِ (اى فى تلاوتِهِ) – تِلْكَ الغرانيق العلى وإنّ شفاعتهنّ لترتجي – فلمّا ختم السّورةَ سجد صلعم وسجد معهُ المشركون لتوهّمهم أنّهُ ذكر آلهتهم بخيرٍ – وفشى ذٰلك بالنّاس واظهرهُ الشيطان حتّىٰ بلغ ارض الحبشة و مَنْ بها مِن المسلمين عُثمان ابن مظعون واصحابه وتحدّثوا أنّ اهل مكّة قد اسلموا كُلّهم وصلّوا مَعهُ صلعم وقد امن المسلمون بمكّة فاقبلوا سراعاً مِن الحبشة

Another form of the story is given in the same book in these words :—

وكذا نبه على ثبوت اصلها شيخ الاسلام والحافظ ابو الفضل الاسقلانى فقال اخرج ابن ابى حاتم والطّبرى وابن المنذر من طرق عن شعبة عن ابى بشر عن سعيد بن جبير – قال – قراء رسول الله صلعم بمكّة والنّجم فلمّا بلغ افرائيتم اللات والعزّىٰ ومناة الثالثة الاخرىٰ القىٰ الشيطان علىٰ لسانه – تلك الغرانيق العلىٰ وانّ شفاعتهنّ لترتجى – فقال المشركون ما ذكر آلهتنا بخير قبل اليوم فسجد وسجدوا فنزلت هذه الآية – وما ارسلنا من قبلك من رسول ولا نبيّ الّا اذا تمنّىٰ القىٰ الشيطان فى امنيته (الآية)

This story is also related in much the same way by Ibn Isḥâq, and it is accepted by Ibn Hishâm, the amplifier of his account of Muḥammad's life (*Sîratu'r Rasûl*, vol. i. pp. 127 sqq.). Ṭabarî and others also give the tale as true, as do the commentators Yaḥya' and Jalâlu'ddîn, and also Baiḍâwî, in commenting on Sûrah Al Ḥajj (Sûrah XXII.), v. 51, the verse quoted at the mad's time (even those who were most bitterly opposed to him in Mecca, and who had forced most of his early disciples to flee to Abyssinia to save their lives) joined with him in worshipping God Most High (Allâh Ta'âla'), when he for a time seemed to withdraw his opposition to their honouring their inferior deities also. He went one day, we are told, to pray in the Ka'bah, the great national sanctuary at Mecca, of which his family had been at one time the guardians. There he began to repeat Sûrah An Najm (Sûrah LIII.). When he had recited the nineteenth and twentieth verses, "Have ye not then seen Al-Lât and Al-'Uzza' and Manâh, the other, the third?" it is stated that Satan impelled him to add the words, "These are the Exalted Beauties, and verily their intercession may indeed be hoped for." On hearing these words all the Arabs present joined him in worship, and the rumour spread everywhere that they had all embraced Islâm. The story is well authenticated and is most probably true. But in any case its very existence shows that the opponents of Muḥammad found no difficulty in accepting his teaching as to the existence and supremacy of Allâh, and that they worshipped the inferior deities as

end of the above extract. Al Ghazâlî, Baihaqî, and others fiercely deny the truth of their prophet's fall into approval of idolatry, even for a moment. But, unless the story be true, it is difficult to account for its acceptance by the above authorities; and the verse we have just referred to seems to require the story to explain it.

intercessors with Him. It is but fair to add that Muḥammad soon withdrew the words which acknowledged the existence and influence of these goddesses, substituting for them those now found in the Sûrah, "Have ye male (issue), and hath He (i. e. God) female? That indeed were an unfair division. They are nought but names, which ye and your fathers have named [1]."

Ibn Isḥâq, Ibn Hishâm and Arabic writers in general state that the Arabs, and in particular those that boasted descent from Ishmael, were at first worshippers of God alone, and that, though after a time they fell away into idolatry and polytheism —if the word may be applied to such religious ideas and practices as those which we have described— they nevertheless always remembered that God Most High was superior to and Ruler over all the inferior objects of their worship.

When we come to consider the influence which Jewish and Christian tenets exercised over the mind of Muḥammad, we shall see that these religions no doubt strengthened his belief in Monotheism. But it was not a new belief among the Arabs of the time, since, as we have seen, they had always admitted it, at least in theory. Yet the inferior deities whom they worshipped were very numerous, for it is said that there were no fewer than 360 idols in the Ka'bah, which had become

[1] Sûrah LIII., An Najm, 21, 22, 23.

a kind of national Pantheon. There can be little doubt, moreover, that these local and tribal deities —for such they were—had in practice cast entirely into the shade among the great mass of the people the worship of "God Most High."

It should, however, be noticed that, rightly or wrongly, the earliest Arabian historians assert that the "association of partners with God" was of comparatively recent origin in those parts of Arabia when Islâm arose. Tradition[1], said to rest on Muḥammad's authority, informs us that idolatry had been introduced from Syria, and gives us the names of those who were chiefly instrumental in introducing it. This is stated to have occurred only about fifteen generations before Muḥammad. An exception to this must be made in the case of the veneration paid to sacred stones. This was common among the people of Palestine in the patriarchal period, and was doubtless of immemorial antiquity in Arabia. Ibn Isḥâq[2] endeavours to account for it by supposing that the Meccans used to carry with them on their journeys pieces of stone from the Ka'bah, and paid reverence to them because they came from the *Ḥaram* or Holy Temple. Herodotus[3] mentions the use of seven stones by the Arabs when taking solemn oaths. The honour, almost amounting to worship, still paid by Muslim pilgrims to the famous meteoric *Ḥajaru'l Aswad* or

[1] *Sîratu'r Rasûl*, pp. 27 sqq. [2] Ibid.
[3] Herodotus III. 8, quoted above, p. 32.

Black Stone, which is built into the wall of the Ka'bah, is one of the many Islâmic customs which have been derived from those of the Arabs who lived long before Muḥammad's time. The kiss which the pious Muḥammadan pilgrim bestows on it is a survival of the old practice, which was a form of worship in Arabia as in many other lands. Many tales were told regarding this stone in pre-Muḥammadan times, and these are still firmly believed. A Tradition relates that it descended from Paradise, and was originally of a pure white colour, but has become black through the sins of mankind, or, according to another account, through contact with the lips of one ceremonially impure. As it is now known to be of meteoric origin, part of the story is readily accounted for.

Not only in reference to belief in Allâh Ta'âla' and to reverence for the Black Stone and the Ka'bah but in many other matters also Islâm has borrowed from the Arabs of more ancient times. It is not too much to say that most of the religious rites and ceremonies which now prevail throughout the Muḥammadan world are identical [1] with those practised in Arabia from immemorial antiquity. For example, Herodotus [2] tells us that in his time the Arabs used to shave the hair around their temples and cut the rest close. This is done by Muḥam-

[1] Regarding the observance of the month of Ramaḍân as a time of "penance," vide pp. 269 sqq.

[2] Quoted above, p. 32.

madans in some countries to-day [1]. If there is any difference—of which we cannot be certain, since we do not know whether the Greek traveller ever saw an Arab bareheaded—it lies in the fact that the shaving is continued from the forehead to the back of the neck, the hair being allowed to grow, though cut short, only on the sides of the head. Abû'l Fidâ [2] calls attention to the number of religious observances which were thus perpetuated under the new system. "The Arabs of the times of ignorance [3]," he says, "used to do things which the religious law of Islâm has adopted [4]. For they used not to wed their mothers or their daughters, and among them it was deemed a most detestable thing to marry two sisters, and they used to revile the man who married his father's wife, and to call him *Ḍaizan*. They used, moreover, to make the Pilgrimage [5] (*Ḥajj*) to the House" (the Ka'bah), "and visit the consecrated places, and wear the Iḥrâm [6]" (the single garment worn to the present

[1] Some Arabs wear their hair long, as they used to do in Muḥammad's time. There seems to be no religious *rule* on the subject, hence the difference in Muslim practice in different places.

[2] *Hist. Ante-Islamica*, ed. Fleischer, p. 180.

[3] That is, the time before Muḥammad's mission.

[4] See also the *Apology* of Al Kindî, Sir W. Muir's translation, pp. 92, 93.

[5] As is well known, this pilgrimage to Mecca is still incumbent upon every male Muslim who can possibly make it.

[6] Others say that the heathen Arabs used to perform the *Ṭawwâf* (the ceremony of running round the Ka'bah) naked, but that Muḥammad introduced the wearing of the *Iḥrâm*.

day by a pilgrim when running round the Ka'bah), "and perform the *Ṭawwâf*, and run" (between the hills As Safâ and Al Marwâ), "and take their stand at all the Stations, and cast the stones" (at the devil in the valley of Minâ); "and they were wont to intercalate a month [1] every third year." He goes on to mention many other similar examples in which the religion of Islâm has enjoined as religious observances ancient Arabian customs, for instance ceremonial washings after certain kinds of defilement, parting the hair, the ritual observed in cleansing the teeth, paring the nails, and other such matters. He informs us that then as now the punishment for theft was the loss of a hand [2], and says that circumcision was practised by the heathen Arabs, as it still is by all Muslims, though nowhere enjoined in the Qur'ân. This last statement is confirmed by the author of the apocryphal epistle of Barnabas [3], who says, "Every Syrian and *Arab* and all the priests of the idols are circumcised." It is well known that the same practice prevailed among the ancient Egyptians also. Ibn Isḥâq [4]

[1] In Islâmic times this unfortunately went out of use.

[2] As in the Laws of Amraphel (Ḥammurabi).

[3] Περιτέμνεται . . . πᾶς Σῦρος καὶ Ἄραψ καὶ πάντες οἱ ἱερεῖς τῶν εἰδώλων.

[4] *Sîratu'r Rasûl*, part I., p. 27 :—

وفيهم على ذلك بقايا من عهد ابرهيم يتمسّكون بها من تعظيم البيت والطّوّاف به والحجّ والعمرة والوقوف على عرفة والمزدلفة وهدى البدن والاهلال بالحجّ والعمرة مع ادخالهم فيه ما ليس منْهُ

uses much the same language as Abû'l Fidâ, but adds that the customs which he mentions, including that of the *Ihlâl*, had been retained from Abraham's time. This is no doubt true of circumcision: but it can hardly be said that Abraham had anything to do with the other matters referred to, in spite of the Muḥammadan belief that he visited Mecca and worshipped where the Ka'bah now stands.

It is clear, from all that has been said, that the first source of Islâm is to be found in the religious beliefs [1] and practices of the Arabs of Muḥammad's day. From this heathen source, too, Islâm has

[1] Muḥammad has also borrowed certain fables current among the heathen Arabs, such as the tales of 'Âd and Thamûd and some others (Sûrah VII., 63–77). Regarding such stories Al Kindî well says to his opponent: "And if thou mentionest the tale of 'Âd and Thamûd and the Camel and the Comrades of the Elephant" (Sûrahs CV., and XIV., 9) "and the like of these tales, we say to thee, 'These are senseless stories and the nonsensical fables of old women of the Arabs, who kept reciting them night and day'":—

فاذ ذكرت قصة عاد وثمود والناقة واصحاب الفيل ونظائر هذه القصص قلنا لك هذه اخبار باردة وخرافات عجائز الحي اللواتي كنّ يدرسنها ليلهنّ ونهارهنّ

Sprenger (quoted in Rodwell's Preface, p. xvii) thinks that Muḥammad learnt the tales of 'Âd and Thamûd from the Ḥanîfs (see chapter vi of the present volume), and that the latter were Ṣâbians and held sacred the "Volumes of Abraham" mentioned in Sûrah LXXXVII., 19, in which Apocryphal books these tales may have found place. But this can hardly be considered as proved. May not the "Testament of Abraham" (rediscovered a few years ago), of which we shall have to speak in chapter iv, be included among the *Ṣuḥuf Ibrâhîm*?

derived the practice of Polygamy and that of slavery, both of which, though adding nothing to their evil effects in other respects, Muḥammad sanctioned for all time by his own adoption of them.

APPENDIX TO CHAPTER II.

It is sometimes said in the East at the present day that Muḥammad not only adopted many of the ancient habits and religious rites of the heathen Arabs and incorporated them into Islâm, but that he was also guilty of plagiarism in borrowing parts of certain verses of Imrau'l Qais, an ancient Arabic poet. These, it is asserted, may still be found in the Qur'ân. I have even heard a story to the effect that one day when Fâṭimah, Muḥammad's daughter, was reciting the verse "The Hour has come near and the Moon has split asunder" (Sûrah LIV., Al Qamar, 1), a daughter of the poet was present and said to her, "That is a verse from one of *my* father's poems, and your father has stolen it and pretended that he received it from God." This tale is probably false, for Imrau'l Qais died about the year 540 of the Christian era, while Muḥammad was not born till A.D. 570, "the year of the Elephant."

In a lithographed edition of the *Mu'allaqât*, which I obtained in Persia, however, I found at the end of the whole volume certain Odes there attributed to Imrau'l Qais, though not recognized as his in any other edition of his poems which I have seen. In these pieces of doubtful authorship

I found the verses quoted below[1]. Though they contain some obvious blunders, I think it best to give them without correction. The passages marked with a line above them occur also in the Qur'ân (Sûrah LIV., Al Qamar, 1, 29, 31, 46; Sûrah XCIII., Aḍḍuḥa', 1; Sûrah XXI., Al Anbiyâ, 96; Sûrah XXXVII., Aṣ Ṣâffât, 59), except that in some of the *words* there is a slight difference, though the meaning is the same. It is clear therefore that there is *some* connexion between these lines and the similar verses of the Qur'ân.

[1] دَنَتِ ٱلسَّاعَةُ وَٱنْشَقَّ ٱلْقَمَرْ … عَنْ غَزَالٍ صَادَ قَلْبِي وَنَفَرْ
أَحْوَرٍ قَدْ حِرْتُ فِي أَوْصَافِهِ … نَاعِسِ ٱلطَّرْفِ بِعَيْنَيْهِ حَوَرْ
مَرَّ يَوْمَ ٱلْعِيدِ فِي زِينَتِهِ … فَرَمَانِي فَتَعَاطَى فَعَقَرْ
بِسِهَامٍ مِنْ لِحَاظٍ فَاتِكٍ … فَتَرَكْنِي كَهَشِيمِ ٱلْمُحْتَظِرْ
وَإِذَا مَا غَابَ عَنِّي سَاعَةً … كَانَتِ ٱلسَّاعَةُ أَدْهَى وَأَمَرّ
كَتَبَ ٱلْحُسْنُ عَلَى وَجْنَتِهِ … بِسَحِيقِ ٱلْمِسْكِ سَطْرًا مُخْتَصَرْ
عَادَةُ ٱلْأَقْمَارِ يَسْرِي فِي ٱلدُّجَى … فَرَأَيْتُ ٱللَّيْلَ يَسْرِي بِٱلْقَمَرْ
بِٱلضُّحَى وَٱللَّيْلِ مِنْ طُرَّتِهِ … فَرْقُهُ ذَا ٱلنُّورِ كَمْ شَيْءٍ زَهَرْ
قُلْتُ إِذْ شَقَّ ٱلْعِذَارُ خَدَّهُ … دَنَتِ ٱلسَّاعَةُ وَٱنْشَقَّ ٱلْقَمَرْ

وله ايضاً

أَقْبَلَ وَٱلْعُشَّاقُ مِنْ خَلْفِهِ … كَأَنَّهُمْ مِنْ حَدَبٍ يَنْسِلُونَ
وَجَاءَ يَوْمَ ٱلْعِيدِ فِي زِينَتِهِ … لِمِثْلِ ذَا فَلْيَعْمَلِ ٱلْعَامِلُونَ

There seems good reason to doubt whether Imrau'l Qais is the author of the lines in question. They may have been borrowed from the Qur'ân instead of having been inserted therein from an author who lived before Muḥammad's time. On the one hand it is difficult to suppose that at any time after the establishment of Islâm any one would have the daring to parody the Qur'ân by taking passages from it and applying them to the subject to which these lines of poetry refer. On the other hand, it is very customary even in comparatively modern times to quote verses of the Qur'ân and work them into later compositions of a philosophical or religious character, to which class, however, these Odes do *not* belong. It would be difficult to imagine Muḥammad venturing to plagiarize from such a well-known author as Imrau'l Qais (even though, as we shall see later, he did so from less known *foreign* sources); though this may be in part met by supposing that, as these Odes formed no part of the *Mu'allaqât*, they were not as generally current as poems contained in the latter collection were. The account generally given of the *Mu'allaqât* is that, whenever any one had composed an especially eloquent poem, it was *suspended* on the wall of the Ka'bah, and that the poems in this celebrated collection owe their name, which means "The Suspended Poems," to this custom. Good authorities[1], however, deny that

[1] Regarding the *Mu'allaqât* it may be well to quote the following from Abû Ja'far Aḥmad ibn Ismâ'îl an Naḥḥâs (died A.H. 338). He says:—

واختلفوا فى جامع هٰذهِ قصائِد ٱلسّبع وقيل ان ٱلعرب كان اكثرها

يجتمع بِعُكاظ وَيَتناشدون ٱلشعر فاذا استحسن ٱلملك قصيدةً قال

this was the origin of the name, but that is perhaps a matter of little importance. In spite of the Eastern story which I have quoted, the balance of probability certainly inclines to the supposition that Muḥammad was not[1] guilty of the daring plagiarism of which he has been accused[2].

عَلِّقُوهَا وَٱثبتوها فى خزانتي فامّا قول من قال عُلِّقَت فى الكعبه
فلا يعرفهُ احدٌ من ٱلرُّوّاة واصحّ ما قيل فى هذا ان حمّاداً الرّاوية
لمّا رأى زُهدَ ٱلنّاس فى ٱلشّعر جمع هٰذهِ ٱلسّبع وحضّهم عليها
وقال لهم هٰذه هي ٱلمشهورات فسُمِّيَت ٱلقصائد ٱلمشهورة لهٰذا

As-Suyûṭî says very much the same, though he also refers to the story that the verses were hung up in the Ka'bah as possible (*Mudhkir*, II., 240).

[1] This is the opinion of Sir C. J. Lyall, than whom it would be difficult to find any one better qualified to speak on the subject of ancient Arabic poetry. In a letter which he has kindly sent me regarding the authorship of the lines in question attributed to Imrau'l Qais, he expresses his conviction that they are not his, giving reasons founded principally upon the style and the metre. I have incorporated some of his observations into this Appendix, and I owe to him also the preceding note. His arguments have caused me to modify the opinion on the subject expressed in my Persian work, *Yanâbí'u'l Islâm*.

[2] The Rev. Dr. Zwemer, of Baḥrain, however, informs me that he has found the words *Danati 'ssâ'atu wa'nshaqqa 'lqamaru* (cf. Sûrah LIV., 1, *Iqtarabati 'ssâ'atu wa'nshaqqa 'lqamaru*) in the last section of the last poem of Imrau'l Qais in an edition which he possesses. He adds: "A Shaikh taught in Al Azhar tells me that this evident quotation perplexes learned Muslims."

CHAPTER III.

INFLUENCE OF ṢÂBIAN AND JEWISH IDEAS AND PRACTICES.

WHEN Muḥammad appeared as a prophet, although the Arabs had many religious ideas and practices in which they were agreed, they possessed no volume which could pretend to contain a Divine revelation, and to which Muḥammad could appeal when he claimed to be commissioned to lead them back to the purer faith of their fathers. Yet in Arabia there dwelt certain communities which possessed what they regarded as inspired books, and it was natural that Muḥammad and his followers should therefore feel no little interest in and respect for the ideas and rites of these different religious sects. The title "People of the Book," given more especially perhaps to the Jews, but also to the Christians, in the Qur'ân is an evidence of this. The four communities who then possessed book-religions in Arabia were the Jews, the Christians, the Magians or Zoroastrians, and the Ṣâbians. These are all mentioned together in Sûrah XXII. Al Ḥajj, 17. We shall see that each of these exercised a considerable influence over nascent Islâm, but that of the Ṣâbians was by no means the slightest. Hence we begin by stating what is known of these sectaries, who are mentioned again in Sûrah II., Al Baqarah, 59.

Our knowledge of the Ṣâbians is slight, but sufficient for our purpose. An early Arabic writer, Abû 'Îsa'l Maghribî, is quoted by Abû'l Fidâ as giving the following account of them. "The Syrians are the most ancient of nations, and Adam and his sons spoke their language. Their religious community is that of the Ṣâbians, and they relate that they received their religion from Seth and Idrîs (Enoch). They have a book which they ascribe to Seth, and they style it 'The Book of Seth.' In it good ethical precepts are recorded, such as enjoin truth-speaking and courage and giving protection to the stranger and such like: and evil practices are mentioned and command given to abstain from them. The Ṣâbians had certain religious rites, among which are seven fixed times of prayer, *five of which correspond with those of the Muslims.* The sixth is the prayer at dawn, and the seventh a prayer, the time for which is at the end of the sixth hour of the night. Their prayer, like that of Muslims, is one which requires real earnestness and that the worshipper should not let his attention wander to anything else when offering it. They prayed over the dead without either bowing down or prostration, and fasted thirty days; and if the month of the new moon were a short one, then they kept the fast for twenty-nine days. In connexion with their fast they observed the festivals of *Fiṭr*" (breaking the fast at the end of the month) "and *Hilâl*" (new moon), "in such a way that the festival of *Fiṭr* occurred when the sun entered Aries. And they used to fast from the fourth quarter of the night until the setting of the disk of the sun. And they had festivals at the time of the descending of the five planets to the mansions of their dignity. The five planets are Saturn, Jupiter, Mars, Venus, and Mercury. And they used to honour the House of Mecca" (the Ka'bah)[1].

From this account we see clearly that the Muslims have borrowed from this obscure sect not a few of their religious practices, all of which they believe were taught them by Muḥammad at the command of God through the Angel Gabriel. For example, the Ramaḍân fast of the Muslims lasts[2] a month, from sunrise to sunset, though the rule as to the exact moment when each day begins and ends is, as we shall see[3], derived from the Jews. In Persia and some other countries a gun is fired at dawn and sunset to announce the beginning and end of each day's fast during the holy month. The *Fiṭr* feast at the end of the month is still celebrated by the Muḥammadans. They have, as is well known, five stated times of prayer each day, but they have also two other times each day at which

[1] Abû'l Fidâ, *At Tawârîkhu'l Qadimah* (*Hist. Ante-Islamica*), p. 148.
[2] Vide also p. 269.
[3] Vide pp. 127, 128.

prayer is optional, thus having exactly the same number as the Ṣâbians had. Bowing down (*rakû'*) and prostration (*sujûd*) are enjoined in Muḥammadan worship, but not during the prayers offered at burials. Finally we have seen that the Muslims still most highly honour the *Ka'bah*. Of course it is possible that all these practices were common to the Quraish tribe as well as to the Ṣâbians. Some of them certainly were; but, if all had been, it would be difficult to account for the observations made by the Arabic writer whom we have quoted. The supposition that many of these religious customs were borrowed by Muḥammad from the Ṣâbians, and that their religion in general (owing perhaps in a measure to its supposed antiquity) had great influence on Islâm at its foundation is confirmed by the fact that, when the Banû Jadhîmah of Ṭâif and Mecca announced to Khâlid their conversion to Muḥammadanism, they did so by crying out, "We have become *Ṣâbians*."

The Ṣâbians are supposed to have been a semi-Christian sect. Others have identified them with the Mandaeans, whose religion represents a strange medley of Gnosticism and ancient Babylonian heathenism, but has nevertheless borrowed certain elements from Magism, Judaism, and Christianity, though largely anti-Christian as a system. The Mandaeans derive their name from Mandâ, the most important of the Emanations or Aeons in whom they believe. He is said in their sacred book, the *Sidrâ Rabbâ*, to have manifested himself in a series of incarnations, the first three of which were Abel, Seth, and Enoch, and the last John the Baptist. The latter conferred baptism on Jesus the Messiah, who finally returned to the Kingdom of Light after a seeming crucifixion. This latter idea is repeated in the Qur'ân (Sûrah IV., An Nisâ, 156), and will require notice later[1].

Our very limited knowledge of the Ṣâbians and the doubt whether the Mandaeans can be identified with them renders it impossible to say whether their influence on Islâm has or has not been still more important and extensive[2].

We now turn to the Jews, from whom Muḥammad borrowed so very much that his religion might almost be described as a heretical form of

[1] Vide pp. 182 sqq.

[2] The Ebionites, too, seem to have had an influence on the religion of Islâm when gradually taking shape in Muḥammad's mind, which seems at the time to have been singularly receptive and credulous. "Epiphanius (*Haer.* x) describes the notions of the Ebionites of Nabathaea, Moabitis, and Basanitis with regard to Adam and Jesus, almost in the very words of Sûrah III., 52. He tells us that they observed *circumcision*, were *opposed to celibacy*, forbade turning to the sunrise but *enjoined Jerusalem as their Qiblah* (as did Muḥammad during twelve years), that they prescribed (as did the Ṣâbians) *washings*, very similar to those enjoined in the Qur'ân, and allowed oaths (by certain natural objects, as *clouds*, *signs of the Zodiac*, *oil*, *the winds*, &c.) which also we find adopted therein. These points of contact with Islâm, knowing as we do Muḥammad's eclecticism, can hardly be accidental" (Rodwell, *Koran*, Pref., p. xviii).

later Judaism. In Muḥammad's time the Jews were not only very numerous but also very powerful in various parts of Arabia. No doubt many of them had settled in that country at different times, when fleeing from the various conquerors—Nebuchadnezzar, the successors of Alexander the Great, Pompey, Titus, Hadrián, and others—who had overrun and desolated Palestine. They were especially numerous in the neighbourhood of Medina, which city they at one time held by the sword. In Muḥammad's time the three large Jewish tribes called Banû Quraidhah, Banû Nadhîr, and Banû Qainuqâʿ, settled in the neighbourhood of Medina, were so powerful that Muḥammad, not long after his arrival there in A.D. 622, made an offensive and defensive alliance with them. Other Jewish settlements were to be found in the neighbourhood of Khaibar and the Wâdî u'l Qura' and on the shores of the Gulf of ʿAqabah. The fact that the Jews possessed inspired books and were undoubtedly descended from Abraham, whom the Quraish and other tribes claimed as their ancestor also, gave the Israelites great weight and influence. Native legends would naturally therefore undergo a process of assimilation with the history and traditions of the Jews. "By[1] a summary adjustment, the story of Palestine became the story of the Hijâz. The precincts of the Kaʿbah were hallowed as the scene of Hagar's distress, and the sacred

[1] Sir W. Muir, *Life of Mahomet*, 3rd ed., Introd., pp. xcii, xciii.

well Zamzam as the source of her relief. The pilgrims hastened to and fro between Ṣafâ and Marwâ in memory of her hurried steps in search of water. It was Abraham and Ishmael who built the temple, imbedded in it the Black Stone, and established for all Arabia the pilgrimage to 'Arafât. In imitation of him it was that stones were flung by the pilgrims as if at Satan, and sacrifices offered at Minâ in remembrance of the vicarious sacrifice by Abraham. And so, although the indigenous rites may have been little, if at all, altered by the adoption of Israelitish legends, they came to be received in a totally different light, and to be connected in Arab imagination with something of the sanctity of Abraham the Friend of God[1]. . . . It was upon this common ground Muḥammad took his stand, and proclaimed to his people a new and a spiritual system, in accents to which the whole Peninsula could respond. The rites of the Ka'bah were retained, but, stripped of all idolatrous tendency, they still hang, a strange unmeaning shroud, around the living theism of Islâm.

"Familiarity with the Abrahamic races also introduced the doctrine of the immortality of the soul, and the resurrection from the dead; but these were held with many fantastic ideas of Arabian growth. Revenge pictured the murdered soul as a bird chirping for retribution against the murderer; and a camel was sometimes left to

[1] Sûrah IV., An Nisâ, 124.

starve at the grave of his master, that he might be ready at the resurrection again to carry him. A vast variety of Biblical language was also in common use, or at least sufficiently in use to be commonly understood. Faith, Repentance, Heaven and Hell, the Devil and his Angels, the heavenly Angels, Gabriel the Messenger of God, are specimens acquired from some Jewish source, either current or ready for adoption. Similarly familiar were the stories of the Fall of Man, the Flood, the destruction of the Cities of the Plain, &c.—so that there was an extensive substratum of crude ideas bordering upon the spiritual, ready to the hand of Muḥammad."

Early Arabian writers inform us that when Muḥammad appeared the Jews were expecting the advent of the Messiah, and used frequently to threaten their enemies with the vengeance which the coming Prophet would take upon them. This no doubt had its influence in leading some among the Arabs, especially the Banû Khazraj of Medina (as Ibn Isḥâq says), to accept Muḥammad as the Prophet whose advent was predicted.

Muḥammad declared that he was Divinely commissioned not to found a new religion but to recall men to the "Faith of Abraham." It was natural for him, therefore, to endeavour to gain the Jews over to his side. This he attempted to do at Medina, and for some time it seemed as if he had a fair prospect of success. One step which he took at this time shows very clearly this purpose. He adopted Jerusalem as the *Qiblah* of his Faith—that is to say, he directed his followers to imitate the Jewish practice by turning their faces towards Jerusalem when praying. At a later period, when he had broken with the Jews and found it more useful to conciliate the Arabs, he adopted Mecca [1] as the *Qiblah*, and this it has ever since continued to be amongst Muslims. But soon after his arrival in Medina, observing the Jews engaged in the observances of the Day of Atonement, he enjoined upon his own followers the same observance, *adopting even the same name* (in Arabic *'Âshûrâ*) by which it was known among the Jews [2]. The sacrifices offered on this occasion were doubtless intended to supersede those which the heathen Arabs used to offer in the Valley of Minâ during the pilgrimage to Mecca. It was not until April, A. D. 624, after his quarrel with the Jews, that Muḥammad instituted the *'Îdu'ḍ Ḍuḥâ*, which festival is supposed to commemorate Abraham's sacrifice of *Ishmael* (as the Muslims assert). Even thus we perceive the influence of Judaism on Islâm. This festival is still observed by the Muslims. Muḥammad initiated the Jewish practice in offering two [3] sacrifices on

[1] In Nov., A. D. 623 : Sûrah II., Al Baqarah, 136-40.

[2] When at a later period the month of Ramaḍân was appointed instead as a month of fasting, Muḥammad did not forbid the observance of the *'Âshûrâ* on the *tenth* day of *Muḥarram* (cf. Lev. xxiii. 27).

[3] Sir W. Muir, op. cit., p. 188.

the day of the *'Îd*, inasmuch as he slew two kids, one for his people and the other for himself, though he reversed the Jewish order in accordance with which the High Priest on the Day of Atonement offers first for[1] himself and then for the nation at large. In these matters we see Jewish influence at work both in Muḥammad's adoption of their rites when he wished to gain the Jews, and in his altering them when no longer hoping to do so. In the latter case he generally reverted more or less to the customs of the heathen Arabs. . On the Muḥammadan theory of the Divine authority of the Qur'ân, this phenomenon is absolutely inexplicable. It is to the period shortly before, and especially to that which immediately followed, the Hijrah, according to Tradition (in this respect no doubt reliable), that most of those verses of the Qur'ân belong, in which it is asserted that the Qur'ân is in accord[2] with the teaching of the Prophets of Israel, and that this constitutes a decisive proof that it is from God. At that time Muḥammad introduced into the Sûrahs which he delivered a particularly large measure of Jewish legends, as the perusal of the later Meccan and earlier Medinan Sûrahs will show. He soon, however, found that the Jews were not prepared to believe in him, though it might suit their purpose to pretend for

[1] Lev. xvi; Heb. vii. 27.

[2] Cf. e.g. Sûrah XXIX., Al 'Ankabût, 45: Sûrah II., Al Baqarah, 130; &c.

a time to be favourably impressed and likely to admit his claim. A rupture was bound to come sooner or later, since no true Israelite could really believe that either the Messiah (which Muḥammad did not claim to be, for he accepted that as the title of Jesus) or any other great Prophet was predicted as about to arise from among the descendants of Ishmael. We know how the quarrel did come, and how, finding persuasion useless, Muḥammad finally turned upon the Jews with the irresistible logic of the sword, and either slaughtered them or expelled them from the country. But before that time he had borrowed very extensively from them. Even if we do not grant, with some writers, that the doctrine of the Unity of God was derived by Islâm from Jewish teaching, there can be no doubt that Muḥammad's maintenance of that doctrine received great support from what he learnt from the Israelites. We proceed to show that very much of the Qur'ân is directly derived from Jewish books, not so much from the Old Testament Scriptures as from the Talmud and other post-Biblical writings. Although the Arabian Jews doubtless possessed copies of their Holy Books, they were not distinguished for learning, and then, as now for the most part, they practically gave greater heed to their Rabbinical traditions than to the Word of God. It is not surprising therefore to find little real knowledge of the Old Testament in the Qur'ân, though, as we shall see, it contains a great deal of Jewish legend. It is impossible to quote *all* the passages that prove this, but we shall now adduce a few out of many [1].

1. *The Story of Cain and Abel.*

The Qur'ân does not mention the names of these "two sons of Adam," though commentators call them Qâbîl and Hâbîl. But we find in Sûrah V., Al Mâidah, 30–35, the following account of them.

"Recite unto them truly the narrative of Adam's two sons, when they both offered sacrifice: then it was accepted from one of them, and from the other it was not accepted. [The latter] said, 'Verily I shall assuredly slay thee.' [The other] said, 'Truly God accepteth from the pious. Verily if thou stretch forth thine hand upon me to slay me, I shall not stretch forth mine hand upon thee to slay thee: indeed I fear God, the Lord of the worlds. I indeed choose rather that thou shouldst bear my sin and thine own sin, then shalt thou be of the companions of the Fire, and that is the recompense of the unjust.' Then his soul permitted to him [Cain] the murder of his brother: accordingly he slew him: thus he became one of the lost. Then God sent a raven, which scratcheth in the ground, that it might show him how to hide his brother's corpse. He said, 'Ah! woe unto me!

[1] Most of the instances here cited are taken from Rabbi Abraham Geiger's book *Was hat Mohammed aus dem Judenthume aufgenommen?*

cannot I be as this raven and hide my brother's corpse?' Then did he become one of the penitent. On that account have We written for the Children of Israel that whoso slayeth a soul, except for a life or for evildoing in the land, then truly shall it be as though he had slain all men; and whoso saveth it alive, then truly it shall be as though he had saved all men alive."

A conversation, or rather argument, between Cain and Abel is mentioned in Jewish legend both in the Targum of Jonathan[1] and in the Targum of Jerusalem. Cain, we are told, said, "There is no punishment for sin, nor is there any reward for good conduct." In reply to this, Abel asserted that good was rewarded by God and evil punished. Angered at this, Cain took up a stone and with it smote his brother and slew him. The resemblance between this narrative and that given in the beginning of the foregoing quotation from the Qur'ân is not striking. But the *source* of the rest of the Qur'ânic account of the murder is the legend related in the *Pirqêy Rabbî Eli'ezer*, chapter xxi, which may be thus rendered:—

"Adam and his helpmeet were sitting weeping and lamenting over him (Abel), and they did not know what to do with Abel, for they were not acquainted with burial. A raven, one of whose companions had died, came. He took him and dug in the earth and buried him before their eyes.

[1] On Gen. iv. 8.

Adam said, 'I shall do as this raven.' Immediately" (*lit.* out of hand) "he took Abel's corpse and dug in the earth and buried it."

When we compare the Jewish legend with the one given in the Qur'ân, we see that the only difference is that in the former the raven taught *Adam* how to bury the body, whereas in the Qur'ân it is *Cain* who is said to have been thus taught. It is clear also that the passage in the Qur'ân is not a literal translation from one or more Jewish books, but is rather, as we might expect, a free reproduction of the story as told to Muḥammad by some of his Jewish friends, of whom early Arabian accounts mention the names[1] of several. This explains the mistake that the Qur'ân makes in attributing the burial to Cain instead of to Adam. We shall notice similar phenomena throughout the whole series of these excerpts. It is hardly probable that these slight divergences were purposely made by Muḥammad, though it is quite possible that the Jews who related the legends to him had learnt them orally themselves, and that they and not the Arabian prophet made the mistake. That is a matter of small moment. What is certain is that we can here, and in very many other instances, trace the account which Muḥammad gives to earlier Jewish written sources.

What is recorded in the thirty-fifth verse of the Sûrah quoted above seems to have no immediate

[1] Vide pp. 133–5.

relation to the preceding part of the passage. A link is evidently missing. If, however, we turn to Mishnâh Sanhedrîn (chapter iv. § 5), we find the whole matter fully stated, so that the connexion which exists between the verse above mentioned and the narrative of the murder of Abel becomes clear. For the Jewish commentator, in commenting on the words which the Pentateuch tells us God spoke to Cain, "What[1] hast thou done? The voice of thy brother's blood crieth unto me from the ground,"—in which passage the word blood is in the *plural* in Hebrew because it denotes blood shed by violence,—writes thus: "Concerning Cain who slew his brother, we have found that it is said concerning him, 'The voice of thy brother's *bloods* crieth.' He saith not, 'Thy brother's *blood*' but 'Thy brother's *bloods*,'—his blood and the blood of his descendants. On this account was Adam created alone, to teach thee that everyone who destroyeth one soul out of Israel, the Scripture reckoneth it unto him as if he had destroyed the whole world; and everyone who preserveth alive one soul out of Israel, the Scripture reckoneth it unto him as if he had preserved alive the whole world." We are not concerned with the correctness or otherwise of this fanciful exposition of the sacred text, but it is of importance to notice that the thirty-fifth verse of Sûrah Al Mâidah is an almost literal translation of part of this extract.

[1] Gen. iv. 10.

The former part of the passage as it stands in the Mishnâh is omitted in the Qur'ân, possibly because it was not fully understood by Muḥammad or his informant. But when it is supplied, the connexion between verse thirty-five and the preceding verses becomes clear[1].

2. *Story of Abraham's deliverance from the fire which Nimrod made to destroy him.*

This narrative is not found detailed in one consecutive passage of the Qur'ân, but it is related in a fragmentary manner in a number of different Sûrahs[2]. Hence Muḥammadans have found it useful to collect these passages and to form them into a consecutive whole by supplying connecting passages in the way that we find it done in such books as the *'Arâisu'l Majâlis* or the *Qiṣaṣu'l Anbiyâ*. Such connecting links are supplied from the Traditions of Muḥammad. When we compare the narrative thus current among and accepted by all Muslims with the account of the same legendary

[1] The Jewish narrative quoted above from the *Pirqêy Rabbi Eli'ezer* contains the expression *miyyâdh* ("out of hand") for "immediately." This expression (in Arabic عَنْ يَدٍ) occurs also in the Arabic in Sûrah IX., At Taubah, 29, "until they give the tribute *out of hand*," where it has puzzled commentators.

[2] In Sûrahs Al Baqarah (II., 260), Al An'âm (VI., 74–84), Al Anbiyâ (XXI., 52–72), Maryam (XIX., 42–50), Ash Shu'arâ (XXVI., 69–79), Al 'Ankabût (XXIX., 15, 16), Aṣ Ṣâffât (XXXVII., 81–95), Az Zukhruf (XLIII., 25–7), Al Mumtâḥinah (LX., 4), &c.

occurrence which is contained in the Midrâsh Rabbâ of the Jews, it becomes clear that the latter is the source of the Muḥammadan account. That the reader may perceive this, we translate first the story as related by Muḥammadan writers, and then turn to the shorter and simpler narrative of Jewish traditionists. Passages from the Qur'ân which are incorporated into the Arabic account are here put in italics. We begin with an extract from Abû'l Fidâ:—

"Âzar, Abraham's father," he says[1], "used to make idols, and he used to give them to Abraham that he might sell them. Abraham, however, used to say, 'Who will buy what will injure him and will not benefit him?' Afterwards, when God Most High commanded Abraham to summon his people to Monotheism, he invited his father; however, he refused. And he invited his people. Accordingly, when the matter got abroad concerning him and reached Nimrod, son of Cush, who was king of that country, . . . Nimrod accordingly took Abraham, the Friend [of God], and threw him into a great fire. Then the fire became cool and safe unto him, and Abraham came forth from the fire after some days. Then certain men of his people believed on him."

This is the shortest Arabic account we have. We proceed to translate the most important part

[1] *Historia Ante-Islamica* (ed. Fleischer, Leipzig, 1831). Abûl' Fidâ was born A. H. 672.

of the narrative given in the *'Arâisu'l Majâlis*. There we read that Abraham was brought up in a cave without any knowledge of the true God. One night he came forth and beheld the glory of the stars, and was so impressed that he resolved to acknowledge them as his gods. The account then proceeds as follows, incorporating as many as possible of the passages of the Qur'ân which deal with the subject:—

"*When therefore the night overshadowed him he saw a star. He said, 'This is my Lord.' Then when it set, he said, 'I love not those that set.' Then when he saw the moon rising, he said, 'This is my Lord.' And when it set, he said, 'Verily, if my Lord guide me not I shall assuredly be of the people who go astray.' Then when he saw the sun rising, he said, 'This is my Lord, this is greater,'* for he saw that its light was grander. *When therefore it set, he said, 'O my people! verily I am guiltless of the polytheism which you hold, verily I turn my face to Him who hath formed the heavens and the earth, as a Ḥanîf*[1], *and I am not one of the polytheists*[2].' They say his father used to make idols. When, therefore, he associated Abraham with himself, he began to make the idols and to give them over to Abraham to sell. Abraham (Peace be upon him!) therefore goes off with them and cries aloud, 'Who will buy what injures and does not benefit?'

[1] This term will be explained in Chapter vi.

[2] The italicized passages are from Sûrah VI., Al An'âm, 76–9.

Hence no one purchases from him. When therefore they proved unsaleable to him, he took them to a river. Then he smote them on the head and said to them, 'Drink, my bad bargain!' in mockery of his people and of their false religion and ignorance, to such an extent that his reviling and mocking them became notorious among his people and the inhabitants of his town. Therefore his people disputed with him in regard to his religion. Then he said to them, '*Do ye dispute with me about God? and He hath guided me,*' &c. . . . *And that was Our reasoning which We brought to Abraham against his people: We raise (many) steps whomsoever We will; verily thy Lord is all-wise and all-knowing*[1]. So that he vanquished and overcame them. Then verily Abraham invited his father Âzar to embrace his religion. Accordingly he said, '*O my father, why dost thou worship that which heareth not nor seeth nor doth profit thee at all?*[2]' &c. Then his father refused assent to that to which Abraham invited him. Thereupon verily Abraham proclaimed aloud to his people his abjuration of their worship, and declared his own religion. He said therefore, '*Have ye then seen that which ye worship, ye and your fathers the ancients? for verily they are hostile to me, except the Lord of the worlds*[3].' They said, 'Whom then dost thou worship?' He said, 'The Lord of

[1] Sûrah VI., Al An'âm, 80–3.
[2] Sûrah XIX., Maryam, 43.
[3] Sûrah XXVI., Ash Shu'arâ, 75–7.

the worlds.' They said, 'Thou meanest Nimrod.' Then said he, 'No! Him who has created me, and who therefore guideth me,' &c. That matter accordingly was spread abroad until it reached the tyrant Nimrod. Then he called him and said to him, 'O Abraham, hast thou seen thy God, who hath sent thee, and to whose worship thou dost invite men, and whose power thou recordest and on account thereof dost magnify Him above all other? What is He?' *Abraham said, 'My Lord is He who preserveth alive and causeth to die.'* Nimrod said, '*I preserve alive and cause to die.*' Abraham said, 'How dost thou preserve alive and cause to die?' He said, 'I take two men to whom death is due in my jurisdiction, then I slay one of them, thus I have caused him to die; next I pardon the other and let him go, thus I have preserved him alive.' Accordingly Abraham said unto him thereupon, '*Verily God bringeth the sun from the East, do thou therefore bring it from the West*[1].' Thereupon Nimrod was confounded and gave him no answer."

The story goes on to inform us that the custom of the tribe to which Abraham belonged was to hold a great festival once every year, during which everyone for a time went out of the city. (This may contain a confused reference to the Jewish Feast of Tabernacles, for the *forte* of the Qur'ân is undoubtedly the number of its anachronisms, and Muḥammadan tales regarding the patriarchs

[1] Sûrah II., Al Baqarah, 26

and prophets are in general distinguished by the same characteristic.) Before leaving the city, we are told, the citizens "had made some food ready. Accordingly th[illegible]ed it before the gods, and said, 'When i[illegible] be time for us to return, we shall return, and the gods will have blessed our food, and we shall eat.' When therefore Abraham[1] beheld the idols and the food which was before them, he said unto them in mockery, '*Will ye not eat?*' And when they did not answer him, he said, '*What is the matter with you? will ye not speak?*' *Then he turned upon them, striking a blow with his right hand*[2], and he began to dash them in pieces with an axe which he held in his hand, until there remained none but the biggest idol, on the neck of which he hung the axe. Then he went out. Such then is the statement of the Honoured and Glorified One: '*So he broke them in pieces, except the largest of them, that perchance they might come back to it*' (and find what it had done[3]). When therefore the people came from their festival to the house of their gods, and saw them in that condition, *they said*, '*Who hath done this to our gods? verily he is one of the unjust.*' *They said*, '*We heard a youth who is called Abraham make mention of them.* It is he, we think, that hath done this.' Then that

[1] He had remained at home on the plea of being ill, Sûrah XXXVII., Aṣ Ṣâffât, 87.

[2] Ibid. vv. 89-91.

[3] Sûrah XXI., Al Anbiyâ, 59; and Jalâlain's Commentary.

matter reached Nimrod the tyrant and the nobles of his people. They said therefore, '*Bring him then to the eyes of men, that perchance they may bear witness* against him that it [illegible] hat hath done this. And they disliked to a[illegible] him without proof. . . . When therefore they had brought him forward, they said unto him, '*Hast thou done this unto our gods, O Abraham?*' Abraham said, '*On the contrary, this the biggest of them did it*: he was angry at your worshipping these little idols along with him, since he is bigger than them, therefore he dashed them in pieces. *Do ye then inquire of them, if they can speak.*' The prophet—may God bless and preserve him!—hath said, 'Abraham told only three lies, all of them on behalf of God Most High: when he said, "*I am sick*," and when he said, "*On the contrary, this the biggest of them did it*," and when to the king who purposed to take Sarah, he said, "*She is my sister.*"'

"When therefore Abraham said this unto them, *they returned to themselves*; then they said, '*Verily ye are the unjust persons.* Here is this man of whom you are inquiring, and these your gods are present to whom he has done what he has done; therefore inquire of them.' And that was what Abraham had said, '*Do ye then inquire of them, if they can speak.*' Therefore his people said, 'We do not find it otherwise than as he hath said,' and it was said, '*Verily ye are the unjust persons*[1], since ye worship

[1] Sûrah XXI., 60-5.

the small images along with this big one.' *Then they were turned upside down* in their astonishment at this matter of his, and they knew that (the idols) do not speak and do not take by violence. Therefore they said, '*Truly thou knowest that these do not speak.*' When therefore the argument which Abraham had brought against them had confuted them, he said to them, '*Do ye then worship instead of God that which doth not profit you at all and doth not harm you? Shame on you and on that which ye worship instead of God! Do ye not then understand?*' When therefore this argument overcame them and they could not answer it, *they said*, '*Burn ye*[1] *him and aid your gods, if ye are active men.*' 'Abdu'llâh ibn 'Umar has said that the person who urged them to burn Abraham in the fire was a Kurd. Shu'aibu'l Jabâî says that his name was *Ḍainûn*, and accordingly God Most High caused the earth to split open for him, and he was swallowed[2] up therein until the Resurrection Day. Accordingly when Nimrod and his people assembled to burn Abraham, they shut him up in a house and erected for him an edifice like a sheepfold. This is the statement of God: *They said*, '*Build an edifice for him, then hurl him into the flames*[3].' Then they collected for him some of the hardest wood and different kinds of fuel."

[1] Ibid. vv. 66-8.

[2] Doubtless a reminiscence of the fate of Korah, Numb. xvi. 31-4.

[3] Sûrah XXXVII., 95.

The writer whom we are quoting goes on to relate how Abraham was cast into the fire but came forth safe and well. He concludes his narrative thus: "And it is recorded in Tradition that Abraham was preserved through saying, '*God is sufficient for me*[1],' and '*He is an excellent Guardian*[2].' God said, '*O fire, become cool and safe unto Abraham*[3].'"

We now proceed to compare with this narrative that which is contained in the Midrâsh Rabbâ of the Jews. There the tale runs thus[4]:—

"Terah was a maker of idols. Once he went out somewhere, and seated Abraham as salesman in place of himself. A person would come, wishing to purchase, and Abraham would say to him, 'How old art thou?' and he (the other) would say to him, 'Fifty' or 'Sixty years.' And he (Abraham) would say unto him, 'Woe to that man who is sixty years of age, and wisheth to worship a thing a few days old!' And he (the other) would become ashamed and would go his way. Once a woman came, carrying in her hand a plate of wheaten flour. She said to him, 'Here! set this before them.' He arose, took a staff in his hand, and broke them all in pieces; then he gave the staff into the hand of the one that was biggest among them. When his father came, he said to him, 'Who has done this unto them?' He (Abraham) said to him, 'What is

[1] Sûrah XXXIX., 39.

[2] Sûrah III., 167.

[3] Sûrah XXI., 69.

[4] Midrâsh Rabbâ, Chapter xvii, in explanation of Gen. xv. 7.

hidden from thee? A woman came, bringing with her a plate of wheaten flour, and said to me, "Here! set this before them." I set it before them. This one said, "I shall eat first," and that one said, "I shall eat first." This one, which is the biggest among them, arose, took a staff, and broke them.' He (the father) said to him, 'Why dost thou tell me a fable? Do these understand?' He (Abraham) said to him, 'And do not thine ears hear what thy lip speaketh?' He (Terah) seized him and delivered him over to Nimrod. He (Nimrod) said to him, 'Let us worship the fire.' Abraham said unto him, 'And let us worship the waters which extinguish the fire.' Nimrod said to him, 'Let us worship the waters.' He (Abraham) said to him, 'If so, let us worship the cloud which brings the waters.' He (Nimrod) said to him, 'Let us worship the cloud.' He (Abraham) said to him, 'If so, let us worship the wind that drives away the cloud.' He (Nimrod) said unto him, 'Let us worship the wind.' He (Abraham) said to him, 'And let us worship man who resisteth the wind.' 'If thou bandiest words with me, lo! I worship naught but the fire; lo! I cast thee into the midst of it, and let the God whom thou worshippest come and deliver thee from it.' Abraham went down into the furnace of fire and was delivered."

It is perfectly clear that the Muḥammadan fable is directly borrowed from the Jewish, though expanded by the addition of particulars due to Muḥammad's vivid and poetical imagination. But here again we see that Muḥammad does not reproduce an account which he had *read*, but a story which he had heard related orally by the Jews. The hold which the narrative took upon his mind is clear not only from his having expanded the tale, but also from the large number of times that he recurs to it in different parts of the Qur'ân. That the tale was well known in its main outline in his time is evident from the fact that Muḥammad has nowhere thought it necessary to narrate the story at full length. His words in the Qur'ân show that he believed it to be perfectly well known to and accepted by all his followers. It was probably current in Arabia long before his time, as so many other tales about Abraham were. Our object in quoting the story as it is contained in the Midrâsh Rabbâ is not to prove that Muḥammad plagiarized from that work in this matter, but to show that the story in its main details was current among the Jews at an earlier time still, and that either this or some similar form of the fable must have been the source from which the Arabs derived their knowledge of it. It is hardly likely that Muḥammad omitted to verify the tale by consulting his Jewish friends, who would tell him that it was contained in certain of their books, and thus confirm his faith in its truth.

We notice, however, that in the Qur'ân the name of Abraham's father is stated to have been *Âzar* and not Terah, as in Genesis. But Eastern Jews sometimes call him *Zarah*, from which the Arabic form may have been corrupted. Or, again, Muḥammad may have learnt the name in Syria, whence Eusebius probably derived the form of the name, 'Αθάρ, which he uses. Modern Persian Muḥammadans often write the name آذر, pronouncing it, however, just as it is pronounced in Arabic, though the original Persian pronunciation was *Âdhar*, nearly the same as the form used by Eusebius. This word in Persian meant "fire," and was the title of the angel who was supposed to preside over that element, one of the good creatures of Ôrmazd. There may in fact have been some attempt made to win reverence for Abraham among the Magians by identifying his father with this good Genius (*Îzad*) of Fire. However this may be, we are able to trace the origin of the legend of Abraham's being cast into the fire to a simple blunder made by certain Jewish commentators, as will be pointed out in due course.

Before doing so, however, it may be well to indicate the line of argument commonly used by Muslims in refutation of the statement that the detection of the source of this and other similar legends in the Qur'ân effectually disposes of its claim to be a Divine revelation. They urge in reply that such facts as those we have adduced form a clear proof of the truth of their religion. "For," they say, "although Muḥammad did not borrow this narrative from the Jews, but on the contrary received it by inspiration through the angel Gabriel, yet, since the Jews, who are Abraham's descendants, have accepted this narrative on the authority of their own traditions, it must be confessed that their testimony forms a strong confirmation of the teaching of the Qur'ân on the subject[1]."

In reply it is sufficient to state that only ignorant Jews now place any reliance upon such fables, since they do not rest upon anything worthy of the name of tradition. The only reliable traditions of the Jews which relate to the time of Abraham are to be found in the Pentateuch, and it is hardly necessary to say that this childish tale is not found there. On the contrary, it is evident from Genesis that Nimrod lived many generations before Abraham's time. It is true that Nimrod is not mentioned by name in the Qur'ân, but his name occurs, as we have seen, in this tale about Abraham's being cast into the fire both in Muḥammadan tradition and in their commentaries on the Qur'ân, as well as in the Jewish narrative in the Midrâsh Rabbâ. The anachronism here is as great as if some ignorant person were to state that Alexander the Great had cast the Turkish Sulṭân 'Uthmân into the fire, not knowing what a long period had elapsed between Alexander and 'Uthmân, and being

[1] This argument is used in the Mîzânu'l Mawâzîn in refutation of certain statements in the Mîzânu'l Ḥaqq.

unaware that 'Uthmân had never experienced such an adventure!

Moreover, the whole story of Abraham's being delivered from the fire is founded upon an ignorant blunder made by an ancient Jewish commentator. To explain this we must refer to the Targum of Jonathan ben Uzziel. This writer found *Ur of the Chaldees* mentioned as the place[1] where Abraham dwelt when God first called him to leave home and country and to remove into the land of Canaan. Now this city is the place that is at the present time known by the name of Muqayyar. The word *úr* or *úru* in ancient Babylonian meant a *city*. It occurs again in the name *Jerusalem* (still in Arabic called *Ûrushalîm*), "the city of the God of Peace." But Jonathan had no knowledge of Babylonian, and he imagined that *Ûr* must have a meaning similar to that of the Hebrew word *Ôr*, "light," which in Aramaic means "Fire." Hence he rendered Gen. xv. 7 thus, "I am the LORD, who brought thee out of *the furnace of fire* of the Chaldees!" So also in his comment on Gen. xi. 28, he writes thus: "When Nimrod cast Abraham into the furnace of fire because he would not worship his idols, it came to pass that the fire was not given permission to injure him." We see that the whole story rose from a wrong explanation of a single word, and has no foundation in fact. Whether Jonathan was the first person to make the mistake is very doubtful;

[1] Cf. Gen. xi. 28, xv. 7, &c.

he may, very probably, have accepted the idea from others. In any case the result is the same. The story puts us in mind of Cinderella's *glass* slipper. Doubtless it was originally "un soulier de *vair*," not "un soulier de *verre*," the latter substance not being so very suitable for making slippers!

It is not to be wondered at that Jonathan ben Uzziel should make such a mistake as we have pointed out. But it is indeed strange that one claiming Divine inspiration should have accepted the fable based upon such a blunder as literally true, should in many different places introduce portions of the tale into a book which he professed to have received from God Himself through Gabriel, and should have taught his followers to believe it, and to consider that the agreement between the Qur'ân and the Jewish Scriptures (in which he erroneously supposed that the tale was to be found) in this and similar matters was a proof that he was Divinely commissioned as a prophet.

3. *Story of the Queen of Sheba's visit to Solomon.*

Regarding the origin of this tale as narrated in the Qur'ân there cannot be the slightest doubt. It is taken with only very slight alterations from the Second Targum on Esther, which is printed in the Miqrâôth Gedôlôth. Muḥammad no doubt believed it to form part of the Jewish Scriptures, and its absurdities were so much to his taste and that of the Arabs that he introduced it into the Qur'ân (Sûrah XXVII., An Naml, v. 17 and vv. 20–45), where it is related in the following manner:—

"And his hosts (composed) of jinns and men and birds were gathered together unto Solomon. . . . And he reviewed the birds: then he said, 'What (hath happened) to me that I do not see the hoopoe (*hudhud*)? Or is it among the absentees? Truly I shall punish it with severe punishment. Either I shall slaughter it assuredly, or it shall surely bring me clear proof[1].' Accordingly it delayed not long. Then it said: 'I am aware of what thou art not aware of, and I have come to thee from Sheba[2] with sure information. Verily I found a woman who reigneth over them and who is brought some of everything, and she hath a great throne. And I found her and her people worshipping the Sun instead of God, and Satan hath made their deeds attractive unto them, and hath turned them aside from the way, therefore they are not guided aright so that they should worship God, who bringeth forth what is concealed in the heavens and the earth, and knoweth what ye hide and what ye reveal. God! there is no god but He, the Lord of the Great Throne.' He said, 'We shall see whether thou hast spoken truly or art among the liars. Go thou with this my epistle, and cast it down to

[1] That it had a good excuse for absence.

[2] The Arabic form is *Sabá*, since the Hebrew *sh* often becomes *s* in Arabic.

them; then turn thou away from them: then see what (answer) they will return.'

"(The queen) said, 'O nobles, verily to me hath a gracious epistle been cast down: verily it is from Solomon: verily it is "In the name of God the Merciful, the Compassionate! Rise not up against me, but come unto me submissively[1]." She said, 'O nobles, instruct ye me in my matter: I do not decide a matter until ye bear witness.' They said, 'We are men of strength and of mighty courage, and command (belongeth) unto thee: therefore see thou what thou wilt command.' She said, 'Verily when kings enter a city, they destroy it and make humble the most honoured of its people, even so do they. And verily I do send unto them a gift and see with what (answer) the messengers return.'

"Accordingly when (the messenger) came to Solomon, (the king) said, 'Do ye increase my goods? since what God hath brought me is better than what He hath brought you. Nay, ye boast of your gift. Return thou to them: for indeed we shall come to them with hosts which they cannot resist, and we shall expel them from it (the country) humbled, and they shall be small.' He said, 'O nobles, which of you will bring me her throne, before they come to me submissively[1]?' An 'Ifrît of the jinns said, I shall bring it to thee before thou risest up from thy place, and verily I am indeed able to do it (and am) faithful.' He who had

[1] Or "As Muslims."

knowledge from the Book said, 'I shall bring it to thee before thy glance shall return[1] to thee.' When, therefore, (Solomon) saw it placed beside him, he said, 'This is from my Lord's favour, that he may prove me, whether I be grateful or ungrateful. And he who is grateful is grateful indeed for himself, and he who is ungrateful, verily my Lord is rich and gracious.'

"He said, 'Alter her throne for her! we shall see whether she is rightly guided or is among those who are not guided aright.' Accordingly, when she came, it was said, 'Is this thy throne?' She said, 'It is as if it were.' 'And we were brought knowledge before she was, and became Muslims: And that which she used to worship instead of God hath led her astray: verily she is of an unbelieving people.' It was said to her, 'Enter the palace.' When therefore she saw it, she accounted it an abyss, and she uncovered her legs. He said 'Verily it is a palace paved with glass.' She said, 'O my Lord, verily I have wronged my soul, and I resign[2] myself along with Solomon to God, the Lord of the worlds.'"

This narrative omits some details that are mentioned in the Targum and differs from the latter in a few points. The Targum states that the throne[3] belonged to Solomon, and that twenty-

[1] *i.e.* In the twinkling of an eye.

[2] *Or,* "Become a Muslim."

[3] *Vide* 1 Kings x. 18 sqq., and 2 Chron. ix. 17 sqq.

four eagles, stationed above the throne, cast their shadow upon the king's head as he sat thereon. Whenever Solomon desired to go anywhere, these eagles would transport him and his throne thither. Hence we see that the Targum represents the eagles as the bearers of the throne, whereas the Qur'ân states that an 'Ifrît did Solomon such a service once only, and then when the throne was empty. But with regard to the Queen of Sheba and the letter which the king sent her by means of the bird, there exists a marvellous resemblance between the two books, except that the Targum calls the hoopoe a "cock of the desert" which is much the same thing. We here give a translation of this passage of the Targum for the sake of comparison with the Arabic account.

"Again, when King Solomon's heart was merry with his wine, he commanded to bring the beasts of the field and the fowls of the air and the creeping things of the earth and the jinns and the spirits and the night-goblins to dance before him, in order to show his greatness to all the kings who were prostrating themselves before him. And the king's scribes summoned them by their names, and they all assembled and came unto him, except the prisoners and except the captives and except the man who took charge of them. At that hour the cock of the desert was enjoying himself among the birds and was not found. And the king commanded concerning him that they should bring him by force, and wished to destroy him. The cock of the desert returned to King Solomon's presence and said to him, 'Hearken, my lord the king of the earth, incline thine ear and hear my words. Is it not three months ago that I took counsel in my heart and formed a firm resolution with myself that I would not eat, and would not drink water, before I had seen the whole world and flown about in it? And I said, Which province or kingdom is there that is not obedient to my lord the king? I beheld and saw a fortified city, the name of which is Qîṭôr, in an eastern land. The dust is heavy with gold, and silver is like dung in the streets, and trees have been planted there from the beginning; and from the Garden of Eden do they drink water. There are there great multitudes with garlands on their heads. From there are plants from the Garden of Eden, because it is near unto it. They know how to shoot with the bow, but cannot be slain with the bow. One woman rules over them all, and her name is the Queen of Sheba. Now if it please thee, my lord the king, this person[1] will gird up my loins, and I shall rise up and go to the fortress of Qîṭôr, to the city of Sheba; I shall "bind their kings with chains and their nobles with links of iron," and shall bring them unto my lord the King.' And the saying was pleasing before the king, and the king's scribes were called, and they wrote a letter

[1] That is, "I shall," &c.

and fastened the letter to the wing of the cock of the desert. And he arose and went up high into the sky and bound on his tiara and grew strong, and flew among the birds. And they flew after him. And they went to the fortress of Qîṭôr, to the city of Sheba. And it came to pass at morning time that the Queen of Sheba went forth by the sea to worship. And the birds darkened the sun; and she laid her hand upon her garments and rent them, and she became surprised and troubled. And when she was troubled, the cock of the desert came down to her, and she saw, and lo! a letter was fastened to his wing. She opened and read it. And this was what was written in it:—'From me, King Solomon. Peace be to thee, peace be to thy nobles! Forasmuch as thou knowest that the Holy One, blessed be He! has made me King over the beasts of the field, and over the fowls of the air, and over jinns and over spirits and over night-goblins, and all the kings of the East and the West and the South and the North come and inquire about my health (peace): now, if thou art willing and dost come and inquire after my health, well: I shall make thee greater than all the kings that bow down before me. And if thou art not willing and dost not come nor inquire after my health, I shall send against thee kings and legions and horsemen. And if thou sayest, 'What kings and legions and horsemen has King Solomon?'—the beasts of the field are kings and legions and horsemen. And if thou sayest, 'What horsemen?'—the fowls of the air are horsemen, my armies are spirits and jinns, and the night-goblins are legions that shall strangle you in your beds within your houses: the beasts of the field shall slay you in the field; the birds of the air shall eat your flesh from off you.' And when the Queen of Sheba heard the words of the letter, again a second time she laid her hand upon her garments and rent them. She sent and called the elders and nobles, and said to them, 'Do ye not know what King Solomon has sent to me?' They answered and said, 'We do not know King Solomon, nor do we make any account of his kingdom.' But she was not contented, nor did she hearken unto their words, but she sent and called all the ships of the sea and loaded them with offerings and jewels and precious stones. And she sent unto him six thousand boys and girls, and all of them were born in the same (one) year, and all of them were born in one month, and all of them were born in one day, and all of them were born in one hour, and all of them were of the same stature, and all of them were of the same figure, and all of them were clad in purple garments. And she wrote a letter and sent it to King Solomon by their hands. 'From the fortress of Qîṭôr to the land of Israel is seven years' journey. Now through thy prayers and through thy petitions, which I entreat of thee, I shall come to thee at the end of three years.' And it came to pass at the end of three years that the Queen of Sheba came to King Solomon. And when King Solomon heard that the Queen of Sheba had come, he sent unto her Benaiah the son of Jehoiada, who was like the dawn that rises at morning-time, and resembled the Star of Splendour (=Venus) which shines and stands firm among the stars, and was similar to the lily which stands by the water-courses. And when the Queen of Sheba saw Benaiah, son of Jehoiada, she alighted from the chariot. Benaiah, son of Jehoiada, answered and said to her, 'Why hast thou alighted from thy chariot?' She answered and said to him, 'Art not thou King Solomon?' He answered and said to her, 'I am not King Solomon, but one of his servants who stand before him.' And forthwith she turned her face behind her and uttered a parable to the nobles, 'If the lion has not appeared to you, ye have seen his offspring, and if ye have not seen King Solomon ye have seen the beauty of a man who stands before him.' And Benaiah, son of Jehoiada, brought her before the king. And when the king heard that she had come to him, he arose and went and sat in a crystal house. And when the Queen of Sheba saw that the king sat in a crystal house, she considered in her heart and said that the king sat in water, and she gathered up her garment that she might cross over, and he saw that she had hair on her legs. The king answered and said unto her, 'Thy beauty is the beauty of women, and thy hair is the hair of a man; and hair is beautiful for a man, but for a woman it is disgraceful.' The Queen of Sheba answered and said to him, 'My lord the king, I shall utter to thee three parables, which if thou explain to me, I shall know that thou art a wise man, and if not, thou art as the rest of men.' (Solomon solved all three problems.) And she said, 'Blessed be the Lord thy God who delighted in thee to seat thee upon the throne of the kingdom to do judgment and justice.' And she gave unto the king good gold and silver. . . . And the king gave her all that she desired."

In this Jewish narrative we see that there is mention made of certain puzzles which the Queen of Sheba desired Solomon to solve for her. Although this matter is not mentioned in the Qur'ân, yet it is all recorded in the Traditions. And since what the Qur'ân says with regard to the Queen's mistaking the crystal pavement for a deep pool of water is not quite so full an account of the incident as that given in the Targum, certain Muḥammadan writers have filled up the details exactly. For instance, in the 'Arâisu'l Majâlis (p. 438) we read: "She uncovered her legs that she might wade through it, unto Solomon. Then Solomon beheld her, and lo! she was the fairest of women as to leg and foot, except that she was hairy-legged. When therefore Solomon saw that, he cried out to prevent her, and he called aloud to her, 'Verily it is a palace paved with glass.'"

The mention of the crystal pavement may be due to a confused recollection of the "molten sea" in the Temple at Jerusalem (1 Kings vii. 23). All the other marvels seem to be purely Jewish fancies. The Jewish account is so evidently fabulous that it is surprising that Muḥammad so evidently believed it to be strictly true. But some of the incidents mentioned can be somewhat more fully explained than others. For instance, the idea (widely prevalent in the East to the present day) that Solomon ruled over various kinds of evil spirits was derived from the Jews from a misunderstanding[1] of the Hebrew words שִׁדָּה וְשִׁדּוֹת in Eccles. ii. 8. These words probably mean "a lady and ladies." But the commentators seem to have misunderstood the terms, which occur nowhere else in the Bible, and to have explained them as denoting certain demons (fem. of שֵׁדִים). Hence he is spoken of in both the Jewish legend and in the Qur'ân as having armies composed of various kinds of spirits. The story of the Merchant and the Jinnî in the Arabian Nights is another instance of the same belief. It is strange to find the Prophet Muḥammad emulating the writer of that wonderful book as a story-teller, even though the source of

[1] Or rather perhaps from the Persian story of Jamshîd, which seemed to suit Solomon because of the misunderstanding referred to in the text. Vide pp. 249, 250.

the Qur'ânic tale is known. In credulity, however, Muḥammad undoubtedly eclipsed his rival, for the latter cannot be supposed to have believed his own wondrous tales, nor does he profess to have received them from above.

The historical basis for the whole tale is afforded by the record given in 1 Kings x. 1–10 (and repeated in 2 Chron. ix. 1–9), which tells us nothing whatever marvellous about Solomon, nothing about Jinns and 'Ifrîts and crystal palaces, but is a simple narrative of a visit paid to Solomon by the Queen of Sheba, a well-known part of Arabia.

"And when the Queen of Sheba heard of the fame of Solomon concerning the name of the Lord, she came to prove him with hard questions. And she came to Jerusalem with a very great train, with camels that bare spices and very much gold and precious stones: and when she was come to Solomon, she communed with him of all that was in her heart. And Solomon told her all her questions: there was not anything hid from the king which he told her not. And when the queen of Sheba had seen all the wisdom of Solomon, and the house that he had built, and the meat of his table, and the sitting of his servants, and the attendance of his ministers, and their apparel, and his cupbearers, and his ascent by which he went up unto the house of the Lord; there was no more spirit in her. And she said to the king, 'It was a true report that I heard in my own land of thy acts, and of thy wisdom. Howbeit, I believed not the words, until I came, and mine eyes had seen it: and, behold, the half was not told me: thy wisdom and prosperity exceedeth the fame which I heard. Happy are thy men, happy are these thy servants, which stand continually before thee, *and* that hear thy wisdom. Blessed be the Lord thy God, which delighted in thee, to set thee on the throne of Israel: because the Lord loved Israel for ever, therefore made He thee king to do judgment and justice.' And she gave the king an hundred and twenty talents of gold, and of spices very great store, and precious stones: there came no more such abundance of spices as those which the queen of Sheba gave to King Solomon."

Although many others of the narratives that are contained in the Qur'ân have been borrowed from Jewish fables, yet here it is not necessary to quote them all at length. In every case Muḥammad seems to have been ignorant of the true history of the Prophets as related in the Canonical Books of the Old Testament. This was doubtless due to the fact that the Jews of Arabia were not learned men, and that they were better acquainted with the fables of the Talmud than with the Bible. Before we proceed to more important matters, however, we must deal with the story of Hârût and Mârût, the two angels that sinned in Babylon. This legend is of much interest, as we can trace it in the first instance to the Jews, and can then show that it is of composite origin. We first quote it as it is narrated in the Qur'ân and the Traditions, and shall then refer to the Jewish and other legends from which it was derived.

4. *Story of Hârût and Mârût.*

In the Qur'ân (Sûrah II., Al Baqarah, 96) it is thus written:—

"Solomon did not disbelieve, but the Devils disbelieved. And they teach men sorcery and what had been sent down unto the two angels in Babel, Hârût and Mârût. And they teach not anyone until they both say, 'Verily we are Rebellion, therefore do not thou disbelieve.'"

In the *'Arâisu'l Majâlis* we find the following story, told on the authority of Tradition, in explanation of this verse. "The Commentators say that, when the angels saw the vile deeds of the sons of men that ascended up to heaven in the time of the Prophet Idrîs, they rebuked them for that and repudiated them and said, 'These are those whom Thou hast made Vicegerents upon earth and whom Thou hast chosen, yet they offend against Thee.' Therefore God Most High said, 'If I had sent you down to the Earth and had instilled into you what I have instilled into them, ye would have done as they have done.' They said, 'God forbid! O our Lord, it were unfitting for us to offend against Thee.' God Most High said, 'Choose ye out two angels of the best of you: I shall send them both down to the Earth.' Accordingly they chose Hârût and Mârût, who were among the best and most devout of the angels. Al Kalbî says, 'God Most High said, "Choose ye out three of you;" so they chose 'Azz, who is Hârût, and 'Azâbî, who is Mârût, and 'Azrâîl. And indeed he changed the names of those two when they became involved in guilt, as God changed the name of Iblîs, for his name was 'Azâzîl. Then God Most High instilled into them the desire which He had instilled into the sons of men, and sent them down to the Earth; and He commanded them to judge justly between men, and He prohibited them from polytheism and from unjustly slaying and from unchastity and from drinking wine. As for 'Azrâîl, when desire fell into his heart, verily he asked pardon of his Lord and begged that He would take him up to heaven. Therefore He pardoned him and took him up. And he worshipped for forty years; then he raised his head; and after that he did not cease to hang down his head through feeling shame before God Most High. But as for the other two, verily they remained as they were. They used to judge among men during the day, and when it was evening they repeated the Great Name of God Most High and ascended up to heaven. Qatâdah says that a month had not passed ere they fell into temptation, and that because one day Zuhrah, who was one of the most beautiful of women, brought a law-suit to them. 'Alî says she was of the people of Fârs and was queen in her own country. When therefore they saw her, she captivated the hearts of both of them. Hence they asked her for herself. She refused and went away. Then on the next day she returned, and they did as before. She said, 'No, unless ye both worship what I worship and pray to this idol and commit murder and drink wine.' They both said, 'We cannot possibly do these things, for God has prohibited us from doing them.' Accordingly she went away. Then on the third day she returned, and with her a cup of wine, and she showed herself favourable unto them. Accordingly they asked her for herself. Then she refused and proposed to them what she had said the previous day. Then they said, 'To worship any but God is a fearful thing, and to murder is a fearful thing, and the easiest of the three is to drink wine.' Accordingly they drank the wine: then they became intoxicated and fell upon the woman. . . . A man saw them, and they slew him. Kalbî bin Anas says that they worshipped the idol. Then God transformed Zuhrah into a star. 'Alî and Sadî and Kalbî say that she said, 'Ye will not obtain me until ye teach me that by means of which ye ascend to heaven.' Therefore they said, 'We ascend by means of the greatest name of God.' Then she said, 'Ye will not therefore obtain me until ye teach it to me.'

One of them said to his companion, 'Teach it to her.' He said, 'Verily I fear God.' Then said the other, 'Where then is the mercy of God Most High?' Then they taught it to her. Accordingly she uttered it and ascended to heaven, and God Most High transformed her into a star."

Zuhrah is the Arabic name of the planet Venus. The number of authorities quoted for the various forms of this story is a sufficient proof how generally it is accepted among Muslims as having been handed down by Tradition from the lips of their Prophet. There are several points in the tale which would of themselves indicate its Jewish origin, even had we no further proof. One of these is the idea that any one who knows the special name of God—the "Incommunicable Name" as the Jews call it—can thereby do great things. It is well known, for example, that certain Jewish writers of olden times explained our Lord's miracles by asserting that He performed them by pronouncing this Name, the *Tetragrammaton*. Again, the angel 'Azrâîl bears not an Arabic but a Hebrew name.

But we have more direct proof than this of the Jewish origin of the tale. It is contained in the Midrâsh Yalkût, chapter xliv, in these words:—

"His disciples asked Rab Joseph, 'What is 'Azâêl?' He said to them, 'When the generation (that lived at the time) of the Flood arose and offered up vain worship (*i.e.* worship to idols), the

Holy One, Blessed be He! was wroth. At once there arose two angels, Shemḥazâi and ʿAzâêl, and said in His presence, "O Lord of the World! did we not say in Thy presence, when thou didst create Thy world, 'What is man that Thou art mindful of him?'" (Ps. viii. 4). He said to them, "And as for the world, what will become of it?" They said to Him, "O Lord of the World, we shall rule over it." He said to them, "It is manifest and known unto Me that, if ye were dominant in the Earth, evil desire would reign in you, and ye would be more stubborn than the sons of men." They said to Him, "Give us permission, and we shall dwell with the creatures, and Thou shalt see how we shall sanctify Thy name." He said to them, "Go down and dwell with them." At once Shemḥazâi saw a damsel, whose name was Esther. He fixed his eyes upon her: he said, "Be complaisant to me." She said to him, "I shall not hearken unto thee until thou teach me the peculiar Name [of God], by means of which thou ascendest to the sky at the hour that thou repeatest it." He taught it to her. Then she repeated it: then too she ascended to the sky and was not humbled. The Holy One, Blessed be He! said, "Since she hath separated herself from transgression, go ye and place her among the seven stars, that ye may be pure with regard to her for ever." And she was placed in the Pleiades. They instantly degraded themselves with the daughters of men, who were beautiful, and they could not satisfy their desire. They arose and took wives and begat sons, Hiwwâ and Hîâ. And 'Azâêl was master of varieties of ornaments and kinds of adornments of women, which render men prone to the thought of transgression.'"

To what is said in this last sentence we shall recur again later[1]. It should be noticed that the *'Azâêl* of the Midrâsh is the *'Azrâîl* of the Muḥammadan legend.

It is impossible for any one to compare the Muḥammadan with the Jewish legend without perceiving that the former is derived from the latter, not exactly word for word, but as it was related orally. There are, however, some interesting points in the Muḥammadan form of the fable which require attention before we investigate the question, "Where did the Jews themselves learn the story?"

One of these points is the origin of the names Hârût and Mârût. These angels are said to have had other names originally, being called 'Azz and 'Azâbî respectively, and the latter names are formed from roots common to the Hebrew and the Arabic languages. In the Midrâsh Yalkût, however, the angels that sinned are called Shemḥazâi and 'Azâêl, whereas the Arabic legend says that 'Azrâîl, though he did come down, accompanied Hârût and Mârût as a third member of the party,

[1] Vide pp. 107, 108.

and afterwards returned to heaven without committing actual sin. He is now regarded by Muslims as the Angel of Death, a part played by Sammâêl among the Jews. The Arabic legend says that the names Hârût and Mârût were not given to these two angels until after they had sinned. The meaning underlying this becomes clear when we discover that the names are those of two ancient Armenian deities, worshipped by the Armenians before their conversion to Christianity in the third and fourth centuries of the Christian era. In Armenian they were termed Hôrôt and Môrôt, and a modern Armenian writer mentions the part which they were supposed to play in the ancient mythology of his country in these words:—

"Among the assistants of the goddess Spandaramit were undoubtedly Hôrôt and Môrôt, demigods of Mount Masis (Ararat), and Amênabegh, and perhaps other deities also which are still unknown to us. They were the special promotors of the *productiveness* and profitableness of the earth [1]."

The Armenian Spandaramit is the Avestic Speñta Ârmaiti, the female archangel who presides over the earth and is the guardian of virtuous women. Hôrôt and Môrôt appear in the Avestâ as Haurvaṭ (or Haurvatâṭ) and Ameretâṭ, "abundance" and "immortality." They are the fifth and sixth of the Amshâspands (*Amesha-speñtas*, "bountiful im-

[1] *Ĕntiṛ Ḥalouadsneṛ*, pt. I. p. 127.

mortals"), who are the chief assistants and ministers of Ahurô Mazdâo (Ôrmazd), the creator of all good things. In the Avestâ, Haurvatâṭ and Ameretâṭ are inseparable companions, as are Hôrôt and Môrôt in Armenian mythology. The latter presides over the whole vegetable kingdom. In later Persian the names were gradually corrupted into Khûrdâd and Murdâd, and these two good genii gave their names to the third and fifth months of the year. The words are of purely Âryan origin and occur under their proper form in Sanskṛit (*sarvatá* and *amṛitá*—the former occurring in the form *sarvatáti* in the Rig Veda), though they have not become mythological beings. The Âryan legend represented these demigods as givers of fertility to the earth, personified as Speñta Ârmaiti, and as presiding over all kinds of *fruitfulness*. They were holy beings, and their descent to the earth was in accordance with the command of Ôrmazd, as in the Muḥammadan legend. But originally the execution of their mission was not associated with any thought of sin. Borrowing their names from the ancient mythology of Armenia and Persia, Muḥammad confounded them (or his informants did) with the two sinful angels of Jewish mythology. As we shall see in due time[1], he derived not a little information from Persian as well as from Jewish sources, and there was sufficient resemblance between the two origin-

[1] Chapter v.

ally quite independent myths to lead him to consider them one and the same. Hence the strange phenomenon of the appearance of two Âryan genii as the chief actors in a scene borrowed from the Talmûd in its main features.

The girl called in the Jewish story Esther is the goddess Ishtar of ancient Babylonia, worshipped in Palestine and Syria under the name of 'Ashtôreth. She was the goddess of love and of sinful passion, and was identified by the Greeks and Romans with Aphroditê and Venus respectively. As she was also identified with the planet Venus, called Zuhrah by the Arabs, it is easy to perceive that the difference of names in the Jewish and the Arabian tales is not a matter of moment, the mythological person referred to being in reality one and the same.

It is well known what an important part Ishtar played in the mythology of the Babylonians and Assyrians. One of the tales of her many amours must be translated here, as it explains, in part, the origin of the story of the angels' sin, and also shows why Zuhrah or Esther is said to have been enabled to ascend, and did ascend, to heaven.

In the Babylonian myth we are told that Ishtar fell in love with a hero called Gilgamêsh, who repelled her advances:

"Gilgamêsh put on his crown. And for (the purpose of attracting) the favour of Gilgamêsh towards herself, the majesty of the goddess Ishtar (said to him), 'Kiss me, Gilgamêsh: and would that thou wert my bridegroom! Give me thy fruit as a gift. And would that thou were my husband, and would that I were thy wife! Then (shouldest thou) drive forth in a chariot of *lapis lazuli* and gold, the wheels of which are of gold, and both its shafts are of diamond. Then wouldst thou every day yoke the great mules. Enter into our house with perfume of cedarwood[1].' "

But when Gilgamêsh refused to receive her as his wife and taunted her by mentioning some of the many husbands she had had, who had come to a bad end, then, as the tale goes on to tell us:—

"The goddess Ishtar became angry, and went up to the heavens, and the goddess Ishtar (came) before the face of the god Anu." Anu was the Heaven and the god of Heaven of the oldest Babylonian mythology, and Ishtar was his daughter. Here we see her ascent to heaven mentioned, just as in the Muḥammadan legend. In the latter she tempts the angels to sin, just as in the Babylonian tale she tempted Gilgamêsh.

In Sanskṛit literature also we find a very remarkable parallel to the story that is related in the Qur'ân and the Traditions. This is the episode of Sunda and Upasunda [2] in the Mahâbhârata. There

[1] Translated from the original, which is printed and incorrectly translated in *Trans. Soc. Bibl. Archaeology*, vol. II., pt. I., pp. 104, 105, 115.

[2] *Sundopasundopâkhyânam.*

we are told that once upon a time two brothers Sunda and Upasunda practised such austerities that they acquired much merit for themselves—so much in fact that they ultimately obtained sovereignty over both earth and heaven. Then the god Brahmâ began to fear lest he should in this way lose all his dominions. In order to prevent this he decided to destroy his two rivals. The method which he adopted was to tempt them by sending them one of the maidens of Paradise, called Ḥûrîs by the Muḥammadans and Apsarasas by the ancient Hindûs. He therefore created a most lovely Apsaras named Tilottamâ, whom he sent as a gift to the brothers. On beholding her, Sunda seized her right hand and Upasunda her left, each desiring to have her as his wife. Jealousy caused hatred and enmity to spring up in the hearts of the brothers, and the result was that they slew each other. Tilottamâ then returned to Brahmâ, who, delighted at her having thus enabled him to rid himself of both his rivals, blessed her and said, "In all the world that the sun shines upon thou shalt circle around, and no one shall be able to gaze directly at thee, because of the brilliancy of thy adornment and the excellence of thy beauty."

In this fable we find mention of the nymph's ascent to the sky, though the Hindû story agrees with the Babylonian and differs from the Muḥammadan one in representing her as having from the first had some connexion with the upper regions, for the Apsarasas dwell in the sky, though often visiting the earth, and Ishtar was a goddess. The two brothers in the Hindû tale were at first on the earth, though they ultimately gained authority over heaven. In this at first sight they differ from the angels who came down from heaven, according to the Jewish and the Muḥammadan fables. But the difference is slight even in this matter, since the Hindû myth represents the brothers as descended from a goddess, Ditî by name, who was also mother of the Maruts or storm-gods. The resemblance between these various legends is therefore very striking.

We can hardly, however, suppose that the different forms of the story current among all these different nations were all derived from one and the same origin. The Jews, doubtless, borrowed the tale, in part at least, especially the name of Ishtar or Esther and certain other details, from the Babylonians, who had learnt it from the still more ancient Accadians. Forgetting its heathen source, the Talmud admitted the tale, and on the authority of the Jews it was received into the Qur'ân and the Traditions of the Muslims.

If we further inquire how it was that the Jews accepted the legend, the answer is that they did so through mistaking the meaning of one Hebrew word in the Book of Genesis. The word *Něphîlîm*, which occurs in the passage Gen.

vi. 1–4, was supposed to be derived from the verb *nâphal*, "to fall." Hence Jonathan ben 'Uzziel in his Targum took it to mean "fallen angels," and doubtless in doing so he was adopting the then current etymology of the word. In order to account for the etymology the story was in part invented, in part (as we have seen) borrowed from Babylonian mythology by the ignorant Jews, much in the same way that, as we have previously pointed out, a false etymology of *Ûr* gave rise to the story of Abraham's deliverance from "*the furnace of fire* of the Chaldees." Hence Jonathan in his comment on Gen. vi. 4 explains *Něphîlîm* by saying, "Shemḥazâî and 'Uzziêl: they *fell* from Heaven and were on the earth in those days." The myth in the Midrâsh Yalkût already quoted arose from this blunder.

Yet, even accepting the supposed derivation of Něphîlîm from the verb meaning "to fall," it was not necessary to explain the origin of the name in such a way. The Targum of Onkelos acts much more wisely by understanding the Něphîlîm to have been so called because they were men who used to *fall violently* on the helpless and oppress them. Hence this Targum translates the word by one which means "violent men" or oppressors[1].

[1] It is interesting to note that the Samaritan Targum to the Pentateuch (published by Dr. Adolf Brüll, Frankfurt, 1875) practically gives the same explanation. It paraphrases "sons of God" by "sons of the governors." The original runs thus

Others have in more recent times denied the derivation of the word from *nâphal*, "to fall," preferring to connect it with the Arabic word *nabîl* (نَبِيل), which means "noble" and also "skilled in archery." After all, like many proper names in the early chapters of Genesis, the word may prove to be of Sumerian origin, unconnected with any root in the Semitic languages.

As the more ignorant of the Jews were lovers of the marvellous, the story of the sin of the fallen angels grew ever more and more strange and wonderful. At first only two angels are spoken of as having fallen, and this was an exaggeration of the Babylonian tale of Ishtar's tempting Gilgamêsh alone. But in later times their number in the tales current among the Jews grew greater, until at last in the apocryphal Book of Enoch it is said that the angels who fell from heaven amounted to 200, and that they all descended in order to sin with women. The following extract from that book is important as narrating the legend in a fuller form than those which we have previously quoted. It also gives a statement which agrees with one made at the conclusion of the Jewish legend in the *Midrâsh Yalkût* and also in the Qur'ân, in a passage which we shall soon have to consider.

ויעגלי ברי שלטניה ית בנאת אנשה הלא שפירין אנוי . . . : (Gen. vi. 2, 4)
וגיבריה הוו בארעה ביומיה אנון ואף בתר כן דייעלון ברי שלטניה לות בנאת האדם
ואולדו להון אנון גבריה דמן עלם גברי עריפה:

"And it came to pass, wherever the children of men were multiplied, in those days daughters fair and beautiful were born. And the angels, sons of heaven, beheld them and longed for them: and they said to one another, 'Come, let us choose out for ourselves wives from men, and we shall beget children for ourselves.' And Semiazas, who was their chief, said to them, 'I fear that ye will refuse to do this deed, and I alone shall be guilty of a great sin.' Therefore they all answered him, 'Let us all swear an oath, and let us all bind one another under a curse not to give up this intention until we accomplish it and do this deed.' Then they all swore together, and therewith bound one another under a curse." After giving the names of the chiefs of the rebel angels, the story proceeds thus, "And they took to themselves wives: they chose out wives for themselves each of them, . . . and they taught them poisons and incantations and root-gathering, and they showed unto them the herbs. . . . Azael taught men to make swords and weapons and shields and breast-plates, the teachings of angels, and he showed them metals and the method of working them, and bracelets and ornaments and paints and collyrium and all sorts of precious stones and dyes[1]."

[1] Greek fragments of the Book of Enoch, capp. vi–viii, ed. Dr. Swete, who also gives the same passages from Syncellus. In the Persian *Yanâbi'u'l Islâm* I quoted and translated the Æthiopic text, as the Greek had not then been recovered, or at least published.

This account of the origin of feminine ornaments is the same that we have found in the Midrâsh (see above, p. 98). It enables us to understand the meaning and to recognize the source of the following passage from the Qur'ân, in which, speaking of Hârût and Mârût, Muḥammad says that men "learnt[1] from them that by which they separate a man from his wife." He adds, "And they used not to injure any one except by God's permission, and they teach what injureth them and doth not profit them."

It is hardly necessary to produce any further proof that the story of Hârût and Mârût is borrowed from a Jewish source, at least in all essential particulars, though in the names of these angels we perceive traces of Armenian and perhaps Persian influence. We have also seen that the Jews derived their form of the legend from Babylonia, and that their acceptance of it was in large measure due to a misunderstanding about the meaning of a Hebrew word in Genesis.

It may be urged that some Christians understand Gen. vi. 1–4, in much the same sense as the Jews did or still do, and that possibly this view is correct. But even granting all this, it is evident from what a corrupt source Muḥammad borrowed the narrative, which, in the form in which the Qur'ân and the Traditions relate it, cannot possibly be correct.

[1] Sûrah II., Al Baqarah, verse 96, fin.

5. *Other Instances.*

We cannot mention with the same fulness of detail all the other points in which the Qur'ân has borrowed from Jewish legends. An examination of what is related in the Qur'ân in reference to Joseph, David, and Saul (*Ṭâlût*), for example, will show how far these accounts differ from what the Bible tells us about these persons. In most, if not in every instance, the reason of the divergence from the Biblical account is found in the fact that Muḥammad followed the Jewish legends current in his time, instead of the true history of these men as given in the sacred text. Occasionally he has misunderstood the legends, or has amplified them from imagination or from other sources. But the legends already given at some length will serve as examples of all other similar ones.

We now proceed to deal with other instances in which the Qur'ân's indebtedness to Jewish legends is obvious.

In Sûrah VII., Al A'râf, 170, we read, "And when We raised up the mountain above them as if it were a covering, and they fancied that it was falling upon them, [We said], 'Take ye with fortitude what We have brought you, and remember ye what is in it; perchance ye may be pious.'" Jalâlain and other Muḥammadan commentators explain this verse by informing us that God raised up the mountain (Sinai) from its foundation and held it over the heads of the children of Israel in the wilderness, threatening to let it fall on them and crush them if they did not accept the commandments contained in the Law of Moses. These they had previously refused to obey, because of their severity. But on hearing this threat the Israelites received the law. God then uttered the rest of the speech contained in the verse quoted above. The same legend is referred to in Surah II., Al Baqarah, 60, 87.

Its origin is found in the Jewish tractate *'Abôdâh Zârâh* (cap. ii. § 2), where we are told that on that occasion (so God is represented as saying to the Israelites), "I covered you over with the mountain like a lid." So also in *Sabbath* (fol. 88, 1) we read, "These words teach us that the Holy One, blessed be He, inverted the mountain above them like a pot, and said unto them, 'If ye receive the law, well: but if not, there shall your grave be.'"

Perhaps it is hardly necessary to say that there is nothing like this fable to be found in the Pentateuch. It has originated in the mistake of a Jewish commentator, who has misunderstood the words of the Bible. In Exod. xxxii. 19 we are informed that when Moses descended the mountain with the two tables of stone in his hands, he saw that the Israelites were worshipping the golden calf which they had made. Angry at the shameful sight, he threw down the stone tablets from his hands and broke them "*beneath the mount.*" Chapter xix. 17 tells us that while God was giving Moses the Law, the people stood "at the nether part of (or *beneath*) the mountain." In each case the phrase means "at the foot of the mountain." But the wonder-loving and credulous Jews of later times chose to misunderstand the phrase, and the legend of the elevation of the mountain was invented to explain the words "*beneath* the mount." The tale of the holding up of the mountain above men's heads is, however, marvellously similar to a Hindû legend, related in the Sanskṛit Šâstras. It is said that Kṛishṇa, wishing to protect the people of Gokula, his native city, from a severe rain-storm, dragged up from its stony base a mountain named Govardhana, which is styled the biggest of all mountains, and for the space of seven days and nights suspended it on the tips of his fingers over their heads like an umbrella! We cannot suppose that the Jews borrowed this story from the Hindûs, but it is evident that Muḥammad derived the tale referred to in the Qur'ân from Jewish sources, while the Jews were led to accept or invent the story through taking literally [1] and in an unnatural sense the Hebrew phrase "beneath the mount."

This is not, however, the only wonderful story which the Qur'ân relates concerning what took

[1] That we may understand this better, we have only to consider the amount of error introduced into the Christian Church by a similar explanation of "This is My body."

place during the sojourn of the Israelites in the wilderness. Not less strange is what we are told about the calf which they made to worship during Moses' absence. In Sûrah XX [1], Ṭa Ha, we are told that when Moses returned and reproached them for this, they said, " We were made to bear loads of the ornaments of the people, and we threw them [into the fire] : and the Samaritan likewise cast in. Then he brought out unto them a calf in body, which could low." Jalâlain's note says that the calf was made of flesh and blood, and that it had the power of lowing because life was given it through a handful of dust from the print left by the hoof of the Angel Gabriel's steed, which "the Samaritan" had collected and put into its mouth, according to v. 96 of the same Sûrah.

This legend also comes from the Jews, as is evident from the following extract which we translate from *Pirqêy Rabbî Elî'ezer*, § 45, "And this calf came out lowing, and the Israelites saw it. Rabbi Yehûdâh says that Sammâêl was hidden in its interior, and was lowing in order that he might deceive Israel." The idea that the calf was able to low must come from the supposition that, though made of gold (Exod. xxxii. 4), it was alive, since it "came out" (v. 24) of the fire. Here, again, we see that the use of a figurative expression, when taken literally, led to the growth of a myth to explain it. The Muḥammadan commentator in

[1] v. 90; cf. Sûrah VII., 147.

explaining the words "a calf *in body*" in the Qur'ân as signifying that it had "flesh and blood" has only gone a step further, and he does this to explain how it was that the animal could low. Muḥammad seems to have understood most of the Jewish legend correctly, but the word Sammâêl puzzled him. Not understanding that this is the Jewish name of the Angel of Death, and perhaps misled as to the pronunciation, he mistook the word for the somewhat similar "Sâmirî," which means "Samaritan." Of course he made this mistake because he knew that the Jews were enemies of the Samaritans, and he fancied that they attributed the making of the calf to one of the latter. He was doubtless confirmed in this belief by some indistinct recollection of having heard that Jeroboam, king of what was afterwards called Samaria, had "made Israel to sin" by leading them to worship the *calves* which he made and placed in Dan and Beth-el (1 Kings xii. 28, 29). But since the city of Samaria was not built, or at least called by that name, until several hundred years after Moses' death, the anachronism is at least amusing, and would be startling in any other book than the Qur'ân, in which far more stupendous ones frequently occur.

Here, as in very many other instances, Muḥammad's ignorance of the Bible and acquaintance with Jewish legends instead is very striking. It is hardly necessary to point out that in the Bible the maker of the golden calf is Aaron, and that we read nothing of either Sammâêl or of "the Samaritan."

Again, in Sûrah II., Al Baqarah, 52, 53, we are told that the Israelites said, "O Moses, we shall never believe thee until we see God clearly!" and that while they were gazing at the manifestation of God's presence a thunderbolt struck them and they died; but after their death God raised them to life again. This fable also is borrowed from the Jews, for in Tract *Sanhedrîn*, § 5, we are told that they died on hearing the Divine voice (in the thunder), but that the Law itself made intercession for them and they were restored to life. If it is necessary to seek for any foundation for such a fable, it may perhaps be found in the words of the Hebrews in Exod. xx. 19 (cf. Deut. v. 25), "Let not God speak with us, lest we die."

All Muslims believe that the Qur'ân was written on the "Preserved Tablet" long before the creation of the world. This belief of theirs is in accordance with what is said in Sûrah LXXXV., Al Burûj, 21, 22, "Nay, but it is a Glorious Qur'ân in a Preserved Tablet." Strangely enough, they do not believe that the Psalms are of the same antiquity, although in Sûrah XXI., Al Anbiyâ, 105, God is represented as saying, "And indeed We have already written in the Psalms . . . that, as for the earth, My righteous servants shall inherit it." The reference here is to Ps. xxxvii. 11, 29, "The just shall inherit the earth." This is the only text in the Old Testament which is actually quoted in the Qur'ân, though there are some 131 passages in the Qur'ân in which the Law, the Psalms, and the Gospel are named, always with respect, and it is frequently asserted of them that they were "sent down" by God to His prophets and apostles. To most men it would seem evident that a book cannot be quoted and referred to as an authority until after it has been composed, and that therefore the books of the Bible must have been in existence before the Qur'ân. Of course we know from history that this is the case. But we do not find that any consideration of this kind weighs at all with Muslims, who still cling to their assertion that the Qur'ân was, long ages before Muḥammad's time, written upon the "Preserved Tablet." We therefore proceed to inquire what their received Traditions tell us in explanation of this phrase, and we find the answer in such accounts as that given in the *Qiṣaṣu'l Anbiyá* (pp. 3, 4). In giving an account of the way in which God created all things, that work says, "Beneath the Throne (*or* Highest Heaven) He created a Pearl, and from that Pearl He created the Preserved Tablet: its height was 700 years' journey and its breadth 300 years' journey. Around it was all adorned with rubies through the power of God Most High. Then came to the Pen the command, 'Write thou My knowledge in My creation, and that which is existent unto the day of the Resurrection.' First it wrote on the Preserved Tablet 'In the

Name of God the Merciful, the Gracious. I am God, there is no God but Me. Whoso hath submitted to My decree and is patient under the ill I assign him and is thankful for My favours, I have written him (*i. e.* his name) and raised him with the truthful ones; and whoso hath not been pleased with My decree and hath not been patient under the ill I assign him and hath not been thankful for My favours, then let him seek another Lord than Me, and let him go forth from beneath[1] My heavens.' Accordingly the Pen wrote down God's knowledge in God Most High's creation of everything that He had wished unto the Resurrection Day, the extent that the leaf of a tree moveth or descendeth or ascendeth, and it wrote every such thing by the power of God Most High."

The idea of the Preserved Tablet is borrowed from the Jews. In the Book of Deuteronomy (x. 1–5) we are told that when Moses had, at God's command, hewn out two tablets of stone similar to the ones that he had broken, God wrote upon them the Ten Commandments, and commanded Moses to preserve them in an ark of shittim- or acacia-wood. The Hebrew word for *tablet* here used is identical with the Arabic. From 1 Kings viii. 9, and Heb. ix. 3, 4, we learn that these two tablets were *preserved* in the Ark of the Covenant which Moses had made in accordance with God's command. This is the account from which

[1] Cf. Jer. x. 11.

the narrative of a Preserved Tablet inscribed with God's commandments and by His power gradually arose among the Jews and afterwards among the Muḥammadans. From the language of Sûrah LXXXV., 21, 22, translated above, it is clear that in Muḥammad's mind there existed not only one but at least *two* "Preserved Tablets," for the Arabic is "*a* Preserved Tablet," not "*the* Preserved Tablet," as Muḥammadans at the present day seem to understand it. There must therefore be a reference to the two stone tablets which Moses prepared and *preserved* in the Ark of the Covenant. As these were kept in the Tabernacle which symbolized God's presence with His people, it was natural to speak of them as preserved in God's presence. Hence the origin of the fancy that the Preserved Tablets were kept in heaven, and it was not difficult to deduce their antiquity from that belief.

But why does Muḥammad assert that the Qur'ân was written "upon a Preserved Tablet"? To answer this question we must again consult the Jews and learn what they, in Muḥammad's time and previously, thought to have been written upon the two Tablets, which were preserved in the Ark of the Covenant. In spite of the fact that Deuteronomy clearly states that only the Ten Commandments were written upon these Tablets, yet after a time the belief arose that all the books of the Old Testament and also the whole of the Talmud were either inscribed upon them or at least given along with them. When Muḥammad heard this assertion made by the Jews regarding their Sacred Books, it was natural for him to assert that his Revelation too was written upon one or the other of these Preserved Tablets. Otherwise he thought he could hardly claim for it a degree of authority equal to that of the Old Testament. It is probable that the Muslims, not understanding to what the words "a Preserved Tablet" referred, gradually invented the whole of the marvellous story about it which we have quoted above.

To ascertain what the Jews thought about the contents of the Tablets, we must consult Tract *Berâkhôth* (fol. 5, col. 1). There we read: "Rabbî Simeon ben Lâqîsh saith, 'What is that which is written, "And I shall give thee the tablets of stone, and the Law, and the commandment which I have written, that thou mayest teach them"? (Ex. xxiv. 12). The *Tablets*—these are the Ten Commandments; the *Law*, that which is read; and the *Commandment*, this is the Mishnâh:—*which I have written*, these are the Prophets and the Hagiographa: *that thou mayest teach them*, this denotes the Gemârâ. This teaches that all of them were given to Moses from Sinai.'"

Every learned Jew of the present time acknowledges that we should reject this absurd explanation of the above-quoted verse, because he knows that the Mishnâh was compiled about the year 220 of the Christian era, the Jerusalem Gemârâ about 430, and the Babylonian Gemârâ about A.D. 530. But the Muslims, not knowing this, seem to have tacitly accepted such assertions as true, and applied them to their own Qur'ân also.

To complete the proof that the legend about the Preserved Tablet upon which the Qur'ân is said to have been written is derived from a Jewish source, it remains only to state that in the *Pirqéy Âbôth*, cap. v. § 6, it is said that the two Tablets of the Law were created, along with nine other things, at the time of the creation of the world, and at sunset before the first Sabbath began.

It is well known that the fabulous Mount Qâf plays an important part in Muḥammadan legend. Sûrah L. is called Qâf and begins with this letter. Hence its name is supposed to refer to the name of the mountain in question. The commentator 'Abbâsî accepts this explanation, and quotes a tradition handed down through Ibn 'Abbâs in support of it. Ibn 'Abbâs says, "Qâf is a green mountain surrounding the earth, and the greenness of the sky is from it: by it God swears[1]." So in the *'Arâisu'l Majâlis*[2] it is more fully explained in these words, "God Most High created a great mountain of green emerald. The greenness of the sky is on account of it. It is called Mount

[1] Jalâlain's note on the passage says: "God knows best what He meant by *Qâf*."

[2] pp. 7, 8.

Qâf, and it girds it all" (the whole earth), "and it is that by which God swears, for He said, 'Qâf[1]. By the Glorious Qur'ân.'" In the *Qiṣaṣu 'l Anbiyâ* it is narrated that one day 'Abdu'llâh ibn Salâm inquired of Muḥammad which was the highest mountain-peak on the earth. Muḥammad said, "Mount Qâf." In answer to the further inquiry of what this mountain is composed, Muḥammad replied, "Of green emerald, and the greenness of the sky is on account of that." The inquirer, having expressed his belief that the "Prophet of God" in this matter spoke truly, then said, "What is the height of Mount Qâf?" Muḥammad replied, "It is 500 years' journey in height." 'Abdu'llâh asked, "How far is it around it?" "It is 2,000 years' journey." We need not enter into all the other circumstances told us in connexion with this wonderful range of mountains of which Muslim legends are so full.

If we inquire as to the origin of the myth of the existence of such a range of mountains, the answer is supplied by a reference to *Ḥagîgâh* xi. § 1. There, in explanation of the somewhat rare Hebrew word "Tôhû" in Gen. i. 2, it is thus written: "*Tôhû* is the green line which surrounds the whole, entire world, and from which darkness proceeds." The Hebrew word which we here render *line* is *Qâv*. Muḥammad and his disciples, hearing this Hebrew word *Qâv* and not knowing that it meant

[1] Sûrah L., 1.

"line," thought that without doubt that which was thus said to surround the whole world, and from which darkness came forth, must be a great chain of mountains named *Qâv* or *Qâf*. It is hardly necessary to say that geographers have explored the whole world without—as yet—discovering the range of mountains[1] described in Muḥammadan tradition!

We must indicate a few of the many other ideas which are also clearly of Jewish origin that have found an entrance into the Qur'ân and the Traditions.

In Sûrah XVII., Al Asra', 46[2], mention is made of seven heavens, and in Sûrah XV., Al Ḥajr, 44. the seven doors of hell are spoken of. Both these statements are derived from Jewish tradition. The former is found in the *Ḥagîgâh*, cap. ix. § 2, the latter in *Zohar*, cap. ii. p. 150. It is remarkable that the Hindûs hold that beneath the surface of the earth there are seven lower stages, so to speak, and above it seven higher storys, all of which rest upon one of the heads of an enormous serpent named Šesha, who possesses a thousand heads. The seven heavens doubtless are, or at least were, identical with the orbits of the sun, moon, and the planets Mercury, Venus, Mars, Jupiter and Saturn, which in Muḥammad's time were supposed to

[1] Cf. Avestic Mt. Berez (Kanga's *Avestic Dict.*, s. v.).

[2] So also in Sûrah LXVII., 3, and Sûrah LXXVIII., 12.

revolve round the earth. According to Muḥammadan tradition the earth with its seven[1] storys rests between the horns of a Bull named Kajûtah, who has 4,000 horns, each of which is 500 years' journey from every other. He has as many eyes, noses, ears, mouths and tongues as he has horns. His feet stand upon a fish, which swims in water forty years' journey deep. Another authority holds that the earth in the first place rests upon the head of an angel and that the feet of this angel are placed upon an immense rock of ruby, which is supported by the Bull. This idea of the connexion between the Earth and a Bull is probably of Âryan origin[2]. The legend which represents the Earth as consisting of seven storys is possibly due to the desire to represent it as resembling the sky in this respect. It may, however, have originated from a misunderstanding of the Persian statement, found in the Avestâ, that the Earth consists of seven *Karshvares* or great regions, now spoken of as the "seven climes." Thus in *Yesht*, xix. § 31, Yima Khshaéta or Jamshîd is said to have reigned "over the seven-regioned earth." These again correspond with the *dvîpas* of Hindû geography. It was a mistake, however, to fancy that these were

[1] Vide 'Arâisu 'l Majâlis, pp. 5-9.

[2] In Sanskṛit *go* (ox, cow) is used of the Earth in the Mahâbhârata, Râmâyana, &c. The same word in the Avestâ (*gao*, also *gao-speñta*, "the holy cow") is used similarly. Cf. βοῦς and γαῖα, γῆ: Goth. *gavi* (*Kuh, cow*), and Germ. *Gau*, in all of which the same connexion of ideas may be traced.

situated one below another, except in so far as the first of the seven *Karshvares* was a high mountain plateau and the others stood at lower levels.

In Sûrah XI., Hûd, 9, in reference to God's throne it is said that, before the creation of the heavens and the earth[1], "His Throne was above the water," in the air[1]. So also, in commenting on Gen. i. 2, the Jewish commentator Rashi, embodying a well-known Jewish tradition, writes thus: "The Throne of Glory stood in the air and brooded over the waters."

Muḥammadan writers tell us that the Angel Mâlik, who is named in Sûrah XLIII., Az Zukhruf, 77, is the chief of the nineteen (Sûrah LXXIV., 30) angels appointed to preside over hell. So also the Jews often write of a "Prince of Hell." But the Muslims have borrowed Mâlik's name from Molech (Môlêk), one of the deities mentioned in the Bible as formerly worshipped by the Canaanites, who *burnt* human beings alive in his honour. The word in Hebrew as in Arabic is a present participle and means "ruler."

In Sûrah VII., Al A'râf, 44, we are told that between heaven and hell there is a partition called by the same name as this Sûrah, which in fact received its title from the mention of Al A'râf in it. "And between them both there is a veil, and

[1] Jalálain, 'Abbâsi, &c.

upon Al A'râf there are men." This idea is derived from the Midrâsh on Eccles. vii. 14, where we are informed that, when asked "What space is there between them?" (heaven and hell), Rabbî Yoḥânân said, "A wall": Rabbî Akhâh said, "A span." "And the Rabbâns say that they are both near one another, so that rays of light pass from this to that." The idea is probably taken from the Avestâ, where this division between heaven and hell is mentioned under the name *Miswânôgâtuš* (Fargand XIX). It was the place "assigned to the souls of those whose deeds of virtue and vice balance each[1] other." In Pahlavî it was called *Miswat-gâs*. The Zoroastrians held that the space between heaven and hell is the same as between light and darkness. The idea of a special place reserved for those whose good deeds equal their evil ones has passed into other religions also.

In Sûrah XV., Al Ḥajr, 18, it is said concerning Satan that he and the other fallen angels endeavour to "steal a hearing" by listening to God's commands given to the angels in heaven. The same idea is again repeated in Sûrah XXXVII., Aṣ Sâffât, 8, and in Sûrah LXVII., Al Mulk, 5. This belief comes from the Jews, for in *Ḥagîgâh*, cap. vi. § 1, it is said that the demons "listen from behind a curtain," in order to obtain a knowledge of future events. The Qur'ân represents the shooting

[1] Kanga's *Avestic Dictionary*, s. v., p. 408.

stars as hurled at them by the angels, in order to drive them away.

In Sûrah L., Qâf, 29, in speaking of the Day of Judgment, God is represented as saying: "A day when we shall say to Hell, 'Art thou filled?' and it shall say, 'Is there more?'" This is the echo of what we read in the *Ôthiôth* of Rabbî 'Aqîbâ viii., § 1, "The Prince of Hell saith on a day and a day (*i.e.* day by day), 'Give me food unto repletion.'" This Jewish work refers to Isa. v. 14 in proof of the truth of the assertion.

In Sûrah XI., Hûd, 42, and again in Sûrah XXIII., Al Mu'minûn, 27, we are told that in the time of Noah "the furnace boiled over." This doubtless refers to the Jewish opinion (*Rôsh Hashshânâh* xvi., § 2, and *Sanhedrîn* cviii.) that "The generation of the Flood was punished with boiling water." The whole of the statement in the Qur'ân as to the way in which the unbelievers mocked Noah is taken from this chapter of Tract *Sanhedrîn* and from other Jewish commentators. Probably in ignorance of this the commentary of Jalâlain on Sûrah XI., 42, says that it was "a baker's oven" that "boiled over," and that this was a sign to Noah that the Flood was at hand.

If any further proof were needed of the great extent of the influence which Jewish tradition has exerted upon Islâm it would be supplied by the very noteworthy fact that, although the Muslims boast of the style of the Qur'ân and the purity of its Arabic as a miracle and as an evidence of the Divine origin of the book, yet there are to be found in it certain words which are not properly Arabic at all, but are borrowed from the Aramaic or the Hebrew. Among these may be mentioned: — تَابُوتٌ — جَنَّةُ عَدْنٍ — جَهَنَّمُ — حِبْرٌ — سَكِينَةٌ — طَاغُوتٌ — فُرْقَانٌ — مَاعُونٌ — مَلَكُوتٌ — تَوْرَاةٌ. Some of these are derived from roots common to all three languages, but they are not formed in accordance with the rules of Arabic Grammar, whereas they are of frequent occurrence in Hebrew and Aramaic and properly belong to those languages. The word فِرْدَوْسٌ, "Paradise," is taken from late Hebrew, but has come from old Persian, and belongs to that language and to Sanskrit. It is as foreign to Arabic as the same word Παράδεισος is to Greek. Muḥammadan commentators have often found it impossible to give the exact meaning of such words, through their ignorance of the languages from which Muḥammad borrowed them. When we know their meaning in this way, we find that it suits the context. For example, it is a common mistake to imagine that مَلَكُوتٌ (*malakût*) denotes the nature or the abode of the *angels,* since it is not derived from مَلَكٌ (*malak*) "an angel," but is the Arabic way of writing the Hebrew מַלְכוּת (*malkûth*), "kingdom."

Not less noteworthy is the influence which the Jewish form of worship has had upon that of the Muḥammadans. It would be a mistake doubtless to suppose that the Muḥammadans borrowed from the Jews their practice of worshipping with covered heads, that of separating the men from the women in the mosque (when the latter are allowed to take part in public worship at all), and of removing their shoes. All these were probably the customs of the Arabs as well as of other Semitic nations from the earliest times. It is much more probable that the ceremonial ablutions of the Muslims were imitated from those of the Jews, though here there is room for doubt. The practice of worshipping towards Jerusalem was, as we have seen, for a short time adopted by the Muḥammadans in imitation of the Jews, though ultimately Mecca was substituted as the *Qiblah*. We have also learnt [1] that the observance of a fast-month was derived not from the Jews but from the Ṣâbians. Yet in connexion with that fast there is a rule enjoined which is undoubtedly of Jewish origin. In Sûrah II., Al Baqarah, 183, where a command is given in reference to the permission to feast at night during that month, the Qur'ân says: "Eat ye and drink until the white thread is distinguishable to you from the black thread by the dawn: then make your fasting perfect till night." The meaning of the mention

[1] pp. 52, 53.

of the colour of the threads is that the Muslims were commanded to fast from dawn till dark. When the question arose at what precise moment the day began, it was necessary to lay down a rule on the subject, as is done in this verse. The rule is taken from that of the Jews on the same subject, for in *Mishnâh Berakhôth* (i., § 2) the day is said to begin at the moment "at which one can distinguish between a blue thread and a white one."

In every country where Muslims are to be found, they are directed, whenever any one of the five fixed times for prayer comes round, to offer the stated prayers in the spot where they happen to be at the time, whether in the house, the mosque, or the street. Many of them do so, especially in public places. This practice seems at the present day to be peculiar to them. But if we inquire what its origin was, we must again turn to the Jews. Those of them who lived in Arabia in Muḥammad's time were the spiritual and, in a measure, the actual descendants of those Pharisees who are described in the Gospels as making void the word of God through their excessive reverence for their traditions[1]. In our Lord's time these Pharisees are reproved for loving "to stand and pray in the synagogues and in the corners of the streets[2]," in order to gain from men full credit for their devotion. The resemblance between the practice of the Pharisees of old and that of the

[1] Matt. xv. 6; Mk. vii. 13, &c. [2] Matt. vi. 5.

Muslims of to-day is so striking that some of the opponents of Christianity among the latter have alleged this as a proof that the Gospels are now interpolated, since they assert that the verses above referred to are such an exact description of Muḥammadan methods of worship that they must have been written by some Christian who had seen the Muslims at their devotions and wished to condemn them! Nor was it unnatural for Muḥammad and his followers to take the Jews for their models in this matter. They knew that the latter were descendants of Abraham and were the "People of the Book." Hence, attaching undue importance as they did to outward forms in worship, it was not strange that they should think that the Jewish method of adoration must be the right one. Muḥammad, of course, told his followers that he had been taught by Gabriel how to worship, and to the present day they imitate him in every prostration.

We shall mention only one other point out of many in which Jewish practices have very clearly influenced Islâm. In Sûrah IV., An Nisâ, 3, Muḥammad laid down a rule restricting for the future the number of wives, which each of his followers might have at any one time, to four at most. Commentators tell us that previously several of them had many more legal wives than this. The rule did not apply to Muḥammad himself, as we learn from Sûrah XXXIII., Al Aḥzâb, 49, since he was granted as a special privilege the right to marry as many as he pleased. The words of the restricting rule are: "And if ye fear that ye will not act justly towards orphans, then marry of wives what seemeth good to you, by twos or threes or fours." This has ever since been explained by commentators as forbidding Muslims to have more than four legal wives *at a time*, though they enjoy almost unlimited freedom in the matter of divorcing any or all of them, and marrying others to make up the permitted number.

When we inquire the source from which Muḥammad borrowed this rule, and why he chose four as the highest permissible number of legal wives for a Muḥammadan to have at one time, we again find the answer in Jewish regulations on the subject, one of which runs thus: "A man may marry many wives, for Rabbâ saith it is lawful to do so, if he can provide for them. Nevertheless the wise men have given good advice, that a man should not marry more than four wives [1]."

In reply to the argument contained in this chapter and in those which follow, the Muḥammadans have but one answer, besides the mere assertion that the Qur'ân is not Muḥammad's

[1] Arbah Turim, *Ev. Hazaer*, 1. For this reference I am indebted to a note, p. 451, in Rodwell's *Koran*, where it is added "See also Yad Hachazakah Hilchoth Ishuth, 14, 3."

composition but that of God Himself. They tell us that Muḥammad was ignorant of both reading and writing, and that hence he could not possibly have studied the Hebrew, Aramaic, and other books from which we have shown that he really drew, directly or indirectly, much of what now appears in the Qur'ân. "An unlettered man," they say, "could not possibly have consulted such a mass of literature, much of it in languages which he did not know, and which are known to but a few students at the present time."

This argument rests on two assumptions: first, that Muḥammad could neither read nor write: and second, that only by reading could he learn the traditions and fables accepted by Jews, Christians, Zoroastrians and others in his time. Both of these are destitute of proof. An attempt is made to substantiate the former by referring to Sûrah VII., Al A'râf, 156, where Muḥammad is called *An nabiyyu'l Ummî*, which words the Muslims render "The *Unlettered* Prophet." Rabbî Abraham Geiger, however, has clearly shown that the word rendered *unlettered* in this verse really means "Gentile," as opposed to Jewish. This is confirmed by the fact that in Sûrah III., Âl 'Imrân, 19, the prophet is commanded to speak "to the *Ummîîn* and to the people of the Book," in which verse we see that the *Arabs in general* are thus designated "Gentiles." Moreover, in Sûrah XXIX., Al 'Ankabût, 27, and in Sûrah XLV., Al Jâthiyyah, 15, it is clearly stated that the prophetic office was bestowed on the family of *Isaac and Jacob*, not on that of Ishmael. Hence Muḥammad distinguishes himself as "the Gentile Prophet," differing in that respect from the rest, who were, generally speaking, from Isaac's descendants. There is absolutely no proof that Muḥammad was ignorant of reading and writing, though we are not compelled, as some have fancied, to infer that the polished style of the Qur'ân is a proof that he wrote out much of it carefully, and thus elaborated the different Sûrahs before learning them off by heart and reciting them to his amanuenses. This latter *might* have been done without ability to write [1].

But even if, for the sake of argument, we admit that reading and writing were arts unknown to Muḥammad, that admission does not in the slightest degree invalidate the proof that he borrowed extensively from Jewish and other sources. Even if he

[1] But we are not destitute of traditions, whatever value we may attach to them, which assert that Muḥammad could write, and therefore read. Bukhârî and Muslim quote traditions to the effect that when the Treaty of Ḥudaibah was being signed, Muḥammad took the pen from 'Alî and struck out the words in which the latter had designated him "Apostle of God," substituting in his own handwriting the words "Son of 'Abdu'llah." Again, tradition tells us that, when he was dying, Muḥammad called for pen and ink to write directions intended to prevent his followers from disputing about his successor; but his strength failed him. This latter tradition rests upon the authority of Ibn 'Abbâs, and is reported by Bukhârî and Muslim. It is well known as forming a subject of controversy between Sunnîs and Shî'ahs.

could read Arabic, it is hardly likely that he was a student of Aramaic, Hebrew, and other languages. The parallels which we have drawn between certain passages in the Qur'ân and those resembling them in various Jewish writings are close enough to show the ultimate source of much of the Qur'ân. But in no single case are the verses of the Qur'ân *translated* from any such source. The many errors that occur in the Qur'ân show that Muḥammad received his information orally, and probably from men who had no great amount of book-learning themselves. This obviates the second assumption of the Muslims. It was doubtless for many obvious reasons impossible for Muḥammad to consult a large number of Aramaic, Zoroastrian, and Greek books; but it was by no means impossible for him to learn from Jewish[1], Persian, and Christian friends and disciples the tales, fables, and traditions which were then current. His enemies brought against him in his own time the charge of having been assisted by such persons in the composition of the Qur'ân, as we learn both from the Qur'ân itself and from the admissions of Ibn Hishâm and of the commentators. Among others thus mentioned as helping in the composition of the book is the Jew spoken of in Sûrah XLVI., Al Aḥqâf, 9, as a "witness" to the agreement between the Qur'ân

[1] In fact, in Sûrah X., Yûnus, 94, Muḥammad is bidden to *ask* the People of the Book for information to clear up his doubts.

and the Jewish Scriptures. The commentators 'Abbâsî and Jalâlain in their notes on this passage tell us that this was 'Abdu'llâh ibn Salâm, who, if we may believe the Raudatu'l Aḥbâb, was a Jewish priest or Rabbî before he became a Muslim. In Sûrah XXV., Al Furqân, 5, 6, we are told that Muḥammad's enemies said, "Others have helped him with it," and stated that he had merely written down certain "Tales of the Ancients," which were dictated to him by his accomplices morning and evening. 'Abbâsî states that the persons thus referred to were Jabr, a Christian slave, Yasâr (also called Abû Fuqaihah), and a certain Abû Takbihah, a Greek. In Sûrah XVI., An Naḥl, 105, in answer to the accusation, "Surely a human being teacheth him," Muḥammad offers the inadequate reply that the language of the man who is hinted at was foreign, whereas the Qur'ân itself was composed in plain Arabic. This answer does not attempt to refute the obvious meaning of the charge, which was that (not the style of the language used but) the stories told in the Qur'ân had thus been imparted to Muḥammad. 'Abbâsî says that a Christian named Cain was referred to, while Jalâlain's Commentary again mentions Jabr and Yasâr. Others suggest Salmân, the well-known Persian disciple of Muḥammad, others Ṣuhaib, others a monk named Addas. We may also note the fact that 'Uthmân and especially Waraqah, cousins of Khadîjah, Muḥammad's first wife, were acquainted with the Christianity [1] and the Judaism of the time, and that these men exercised no slight influence over Muḥammad during his early years as a prophet, and perhaps before. Zaid, his adopted son, was a Syrian, according to Ibn Hishâm, and must therefore have at first professed Christianity. We shall see that other persons were among Muḥammad's friends, from whom he might easily have obtained information regarding the Jewish, Christian, and Zoroastrian faiths. The passages borrowed from such sources are, however, so disguised in form that it is quite possible that those from whom Muḥammad made his inquiries may not have recognized the imposture, but may have really fancied that these passages were revealed, as they professed to be, to confirm the truth of their respective creeds, at least so far. If so, Muḥammad adroitly employed the information he obtained from these men in such a manner as to deceive them, though he could not deceive his enemies. Hence, despairing of silencing the latter, he finally turned upon them with the sword.

In the next chapter we proceed to inquire what, if any, influence Christianity, orthodox or unorthodox, exercised upon nascent Islâm and the composition of the Qur'ân.

[1] See the quotation from Ibn Isḥâq, pp. 264, 265 below.

CHAPTER IV.

THE INFLUENCE OF CHRISTIANITY AND CHRISTIAN APOCRYPHAL BOOKS.

WHEN Muḥammad arose, Christianity had not obtained any very considerable hold upon the Arabs. "After five centuries of Christian evangelization, we can point to but a sprinkling here and there of Christian converts: the Banû Ḥârith of Najrân, the Banû Ḥanîfah of Yamâmah, some of the Banû Ṭâi at Taimah, and hardly any more[1]." In his youth, we are told, Muḥammad heard the preaching of Quss, the Bishop of Najrân, and he met many monks and saw much of professing Christians when he visited Syria as a trader before his assumption of the prophetic office. But what he saw and heard of the Church had little effect upon him for good. Nor need we wonder at this. "What Muḥammad and his Khalîfahs found in all directions whither their scimitars cut a path for them," says Isaac Taylor[2], speaking of a somewhat later period in words which nevertheless describe Muḥammad's early experience also, "was

[1] Sir W. Muir, *Life of Mahomet*, 3rd ed., p. lxxxiv.

[2] *Ancient Christianity*, vol. i. p. 266.

a superstition so abject, an idolatry so gross and shameless, church doctrines so arrogant, church practices so dissolute and so puerile, that the strong-minded Arabians felt themselves inspired anew as God's messengers to reprove the errors of the world, and authorized as God's avengers to punish apostate Christendom." The Greek monk who wrote the *History of the Martyrdom of Athanasius the Persian*, speaking of the sufferings inflicted on the people of Palestine when it was for a brief space in the hands of the Persians in Muḥammad's time, draws a fearful picture [1] of the wickedness of the professing Christians there, and does not hesitate to say that it was for this reason that God gave them over to the cruelty of their Zoroastrian persecutors. In the Book of Revelation (ix. 20, 21) the prevalence of idol-worship and other sins such as those described by this monk is given as the reason why the Muḥammadan power was to be permitted to oppress the Eastern Church. Speaking of the same time Mosheim says, "During [2] this century true religion lay buried under a senseless mass of superstitions, and was unable to raise her head. The earlier Christians had worshipped only God and His Son; but those called Christians in this century worshipped the wood of a cross, the images

[1] Ποικίλως καὶ πολυτρόπως τὴν ἁμαρτίαν χειρογραφήσαντες καὶ αἵμασιν μὲν ἀνθρωπίνοις τὴν γῆν φοινίξαντες, πορνείαις δὲ καὶ μοιχείαις καὶ ταῖς ἄλλαις ἀναριθμήτοις πονηρίαις . . . τὴν ὀργὴν τοῦ Θεοῦ καθ' ἑαυτῶν ἐκκαύσαντες, κτλ. *Acta Martyrii S. Athanasii Persae*, p. 2.

[2] Cent. VII, pt. II, cap. iii. § I, ed. Reid.

of holy men, and bones of dubious origin. The early Christians placed heaven and hell before the view of men; these latter talked only of a certain fire prepared to purge away the imperfections of the soul. The former taught that Christ had made expiation for the sins of men by His death and blood; the latter seemed to inculcate that the gates of heaven would be closed against none who should enrich the clergy or the Church with their donations. The former were studious to maintain a holy simplicity and to follow a pure and chaste piety; the latter placed the substance of religion in external rites and bodily exercises." The picture of Christianity which the Qur'ân presents to us shows us what conception of it Muḥammad had formed from his own limited experience. His knowledge of the Faith was at least powerfully affected by the teaching of the so-called "orthodox" party, who styled Mary "the Mother of God," and, by the abuse of a term so easily misunderstood, opened the way for the worship of a Jewish maiden in place of God Most High. The effect of this misconception is clearly pointed out by Ibn Isḥâq. In telling the story of the embassy sent by the Christians of Najrân, who, he says, belonged to "the Emperor's faith," to Muḥammad at Medina in A.D. 632, he tells us of the ambassadors that "Like[1] all the Christians, they said, 'Jesus is God, the Son of God, and the third of three.' . . . They

[1] Quoted in Dr. Koelle's *Mohammed and Mohammedanism*, p. 136.

proved further that He is the third of three, namely God, Christ, and Mary." Of course this is not a true account of the language used, but that it represents correctly what *Muḥammad understood* to be the doctrine held by these Christians is clear from the following verses of the Qur'ân: "Verily now they have blasphemed who say, 'God is a third of three'" (Sûrah V., Al Mâidah. 77): "And when God shall say, 'O Jesus, Son of Mary, hast Thou said unto men, Take Me and My Mother as two Gods, beside God?'" (Sûrah V., 116). We can hardly wonder then that Muḥammad rejected the Christianity thus presented to his notice. "Had he witnessed a purer exhibition of its rites and doctrines, and seen more of its reforming and regenerating influences, we cannot doubt that, in the sincerity of his early search after truth, he might readily have embraced and faithfully adhered to the faith of Jesus. Lamentable indeed is the reflection that so small a portion of the fair form of Christianity was disclosed by the ecclesiastics and monks of Syria, and that little how altered and distorted! Instead of the simple majesty of the Gospel—as a revelation of God reconciling mankind to Himself through His Son—the sacred dogma of the Trinity was forced upon the traveller [1] with the misleading and offensive zeal of Eutychian and Jacobite partisanship, and the worship of

[1] Sir W. Muir, *Life of Mahomet*, 3rd ed., pp. 20, 21. He is here speaking of Muḥammad's visit to Syria.

Mary exhibited in so gross a form as to leave the impression upon the mind of Muḥammad that she was held to be a goddess, if not the third Person and consort of the Deity. It must surely have been by such blasphemous extravagances that Muḥammad was repelled from the true doctrine of Jesus as the Son of God, and led to regard Him only as 'Jesus, son of Mary,' the sole title by which He is spoken of in the Qur'ân."

We must not therefore forget that Muḥammad was never brought into contact with pure Gospel Christianity; and it is largely to the false forms which the faith had then almost universally assumed that the rise of Islâm is really due, since repulsion from these prevented Muḥammad from ever really seeking to discover the truth contained in the Gospel, and thus impelled him to found a new and anti-Christian religion.

There seems to be no satisfactory proof that an Arabic version of the New Testament existed in Muḥammad's time. Even in the "Orthodox" Church the Gospel was neglected in favour of legends of Saints, which appealed more to the popular taste for the marvellous. Arabia was a refuge for not a few heretics of different sects; and it is clear from the Qur'ân (as we shall see) that, whether in written form or not, many of the mythical stories which are contained in the apocryphal Gospels and other similar works, together with certain heretical views on various subjects, must have reached Muḥammad and have been accepted by him as true. That he should have believed these to form part of the Gospel, the name of which is so often mentioned in the Qur'ân, is somewhat surprising: and the fact proves that none of his converts were earnest and well-taught Christians, and also that he must have felt far less interest in Christianity than he did in Talmudic Judaism. Those passages of the Qur'ân which deal at all fully with what Muḥammad supposed to be the doctrines of Christianity date "from a period when his system was already, in great part, matured; and they were founded on information meagre, fabulous and crude. . . . We do not find a single ceremony or doctrine of Islâm in any degree moulded, or even tinged, by the peculiar tenets of Christianity; while, on the contrary, Judaism has given its colour to the whole system, and lent to it the shape and type, if not the actual substance, of many ordinances [1]."

Yet at the same time Muḥammad desired to win over Christians as well as Jews to his faith. If they were far less numerous and powerful in Arabia than were the Jews, yet the established religion of the great Byzantine Empire must have possessed some importance in Muḥammad's eyes, especially because, unless the Arabian Christians could be won over, political complications might arise. To what extent this latter feeling may have

[1] *Life of Mahomet*, pp. 143, 144.

influenced Muḥammad, it is impossible to say. At any rate, he appealed to the Gospel as a proof of his Divine Mission, even going so far as to state that Christ had prophesied of his coming[1]. He speaks of Christ as "the Word of God[2]," but denies His Divinity and His crucifixion, and shows a complete ignorance of the true doctrines of the Gospel. Yet in numerous passages he speaks of the latter with respect as a book of Divine authority, saying that it "descended on Jesus" out of heaven, and that the Qur'ân itself came to confirm and preserve it (Sûrah V., Al Mâidah, 52). He records the virgin birth of Christ and mentions some of His miracles, but even here the legendary tone predominates; and Muḥammad seems to have learnt what little he knew of our Lord and His Apostles from very unreliable hearsay. We shall see that the agreement in detail between what the Qur'ân relates on these subjects and what may be found in apocryphal and heretical literature is very remarkable. Here again Muḥammad seems to have had a wonderful talent for rejecting the true and

[1] Sûrah LXI., Aṣ Ṣaff, 6: "And when Jesus, the Son of Mary, said, 'O children of Israel, verily I am an Apostle of God unto you, confirming what was before Me of the Law, and bringing good news of an Apostle who shall come after Me: his name is Aḥmad.'" Aḥmad is the same name as Muḥammad. The latter must have heard of the prophecy in John xvi. 7, &c., and his informant must, purposely or ignorantly, have mistaken παράκλητος for περικλυτός, which latter word does not occur in the New Testament.

[2] Sûrah III., 40, and IV., 169.

accepting the false, just as in the case of the Jewish traditions referred to in the preceding chapter.

We proceed to prove this by referring to some of the fables dealing with Christian subjects contained in the Qur'ân, indicating the sources from which they appear to have been derived.

1. *Legend of the Companions of the Cave.*

The first with which we shall deal is the legend of the *Companions of the Cave*, which is thus related in Sûrah XVIII., Al Kahf, 8–25:—

"Hast thou considered that the Companions of the Cave and of Ar Raqîm[1] were among our signs, a marvel? When the youths betook themselves to the cave they said, 'Our Lord, bring us mercy from Thyself and from our matter prepare for us guidance.' Accordingly we smote upon their ears in the cave a number of years. Afterwards We aroused them that we might know which of the two parties[2] had reckoned unto what [time] they had remained—an age. We shall relate to thee the account of them with truth: Verily they were youths who believed in their Lord, and we increased guidance unto them. And we girt up their hearts when they stood up: then said they, 'Our Lord is Lord of the heavens and of the earth, we shall never call any beside Him God, then had we uttered a boundless lie. These our people have

[1] The district where the Cave was situated.

[2] Believers and unbelievers.

taken gods beside Him, unless they bring clear authority for them: who then is more unjust than he who hath devised a lie against God? And when ye have withdrawn from them and from what they worship beside God, then betake yourselves to the cave: thus your Lord will unfold unto you of His mercy and will prepare for you advantage out of your matter.' And thou seest the sun when it riseth recede from their cave towards the right hand, and when it setteth turn[1] aside from them towards the left hand, and they were in an interstice of it[2]: that is one of God's signs. Whomsoever then God guideth, he is guided, and for him whom He misguideth thou shalt never find a patron, a guide. And thou wouldst reckon them awake, though they are asleep; and We turn them over towards the right hand and towards the left hand. And their dog stretcheth out his fore-paws on the threshold; and if thou hadst come upon them thou wouldst indeed have turned from them in flight, and thou wouldst have been filled with dread of them. And therefore did We arouse them that they might inquire of one another. A speaker from among them said, 'How long have ye remained?' They said, 'We have remained a day, or portion of a day.' They said, 'Your Lord knowest well how long ye have remained. Send therefore one of you with this your coin into the city, then let him see which man of it has the

[1] So as not to touch them. [2] That is, of the cave.

purest food, and let him bring you provision from him, and let him be kind, and let him not inform anyone concerning you. Verily, if they discover you, they will stone you or bring you back into their community, and then for ever ye shall never prosper.' And thus we made it known concerning them, that men might know that God's promise is true, and that as to the Hour [1] there is no doubt about it. When they argued among themselves about their matter, then they said, 'Build a building over them: their Lord knoweth well about them.' Those who prevailed in their matter said, 'We shall surely erect a mosque over them.' They will say, 'They were three: the fourth of them was their dog:' and they will say, 'There were five; the sixth of them was their dog:' a conjecture concerning the mystery: and they will say, 'They were seven; the eighth of them was their dog.' Say thou [2], 'My Lord is well aware of their number: none but a few know about them.' . . . And they remained in their cave three hundred years, and they added nine. Say thou [2], 'God is well aware how long they remained: to Him belongeth the mystery of the heavens and of the earth.'"

To understand this rather hesitating account we must remember that, as the commentators inform us, some of the heathen [3] Arabs of Mecca had chal-

[1] *i. e.* the Judgment Day. [2] Muḥammad.

[3] Others say *Jews*, but this is less likely.

lenged Muḥammad to tell them the story of the Companions of the Cave, if he could, in order to test his claim to inspiration. The story was evidently therefore current among them in some form, perhaps in more than one. There was a dispute concerning the number of persons who went into the cave, and various opinions were stated on the subject. Muḥammad, as is evident from verses 22 and 23 which we have omitted, promised to give them an answer on the morrow, purposing apparently to inquire of some one about the matter. He evidently failed to obtain certain information, hence he left the question of the number of the youths unsettled, and his attempt to get out of the difficulty is not very successful. Nor does he tell the place where or the time when the event is said to have occurred. He ventures, however, to assert positively just one fact,—that the time spent in the cave was 309 years. Unfortunately, as we shall see, even in this he was wrong. He has no doubt, however, that the event recorded in the story really occurred. From the whole style of the passage we perceive that Muḥammad had no written document and no reliable informant at hand who could give him exact particulars of the affair. None the less we possess more than one form of the legend, written before Muḥammad's time: and it is clear that to an oral form of the story he was indebted for the particulars given in the Qur'ân, and not to Divine revelation, as he claimed to be.

The Syriac writer, Jacob of Sarûg, in a homily published in the *Acta Sanctorum*, gives the myth at some length. He died A.D. 521. Other early Syriac forms of the story are known[1]. Most accounts say that there were "Seven Sleepers," hence the name by which the tale is generally known in Europe, but one Syriac MS. of the sixth century[2] in the British Museum says they numbered eight. Muḥammadan commentators[3] on the Qur'ân relate traditions, some of which say that they were seven, others asserting that they numbered eight, a point which Muḥammad practically in the Qur'ân acknowledged his inability to decide. As far as we know, the first European writer to relate the legend was Gregory of Tours[4]. He tells us that in the reign of the Emperor Decius (A.D. 249–51) seven noble young Christians of Ephesus fled from persecution and took refuge in a cave not far from the city. After a time, however, their enemies discovered where they were and blocked up the entrance to the cave, leaving them to die of hunger. When Theodosius II was on the throne, 196 years later, a herdsman found and opened the cave. The Seven Sleepers then awoke from the slumber in which they had remained during the whole time, and (as the Qur'ân says also) sent one

[1] Vide Bar Hebraeus, *Chron. Ecc.*, I. 142 sqq.; Assemani, *Bibl. Orient.* I. 335, sqq.

[2] Cat. Syr. MSS., p. 1090.

[3] Vide Jalâlain and 'Abbâsî *in loco*.

[4] *De Gloria Martyrum*, cap. 95.

of the party to the city to purchase provisions. He found Christianity everywhere triumphant, to his boundless surprise. At a shop where he bought some food, he produced a coin of Decius to pay for it. Accused of having discovered a hidden treasure, he told the story of himself and his companions. When he led the way to the cave, the appearance of his companions, still young and radiant with a celestial brightness, proved the truth of his story. The Emperor soon heard of it, and went in person to the cave, where the awakened sleepers told him that God had preserved them in order to prove to him the truth of the immortality of the soul. Having delivered their message, they expired.

It is quite unnecessary to comment on the exceeding silliness of the tale as told in the Qur'ân, though in this respect Muḥammad cannot be deserving of more blame for accepting it as true than the ignorant Christians, by whom it was so widely spread and in all probability invented. It is quite possible that the story was originally intended to be an allegory, or more probably a religious romance, framed with the intention of showing with what wonderful rapidity the Christian faith had spread, through the courage and faithfulness even unto death of so many of its professors. Be this as it may, it is undoubtedly the case that long before Muḥammad's day the legend had obtained credence in many parts of the East, and even apparently in Mecca it was believed in his time. Muḥammad's fault lay in pretending that he had received it as a Divine revelation, whereas it is as little worthy of credence as the tale of St. George and the Dragon (also probably an allegory), or Cinderella and the Glass Slipper, or the Batrachomyomachia among the Greeks, or the tales of Rustam's marvellous exploits among the Persians [1].

2. *Story of the Virgin Mary.*

The history of Mary, as related in the Qur'ân and the Traditions of the Prophet, is taken almost entirely from the apocryphal Gospels and works

[1] There can be little doubt that we may trace the origin of the Syriac tale of "The Seven Sleepers" to a classical Greek source. It is evidently borrowed from the tale of Epimenides' long sleep, as related by Diogenes Laertius in the following words:—*Οὗτός ποτε πεμφθεὶς παρὰ τοῦ πατρὸς εἰς ἀγρὸν ἐπὶ πρόβατον, τῆς ὁδοῦ κατὰ μεσημβρίαν ἐκκλίνας, ὑπ' ἄντρῳ τινὶ κατεκοιμήθη ἑπτὰ καὶ πεντήκοντα ἔτη. διαναστὰς δὲ μετὰ ταῦτα, ἐζήτει τὸ πρόβατον, νομίζων ἐπ' ὀλίγον κεκοιμῆσθαι. ὡς δὲ οὐχ εὕρισκε, παρεγένετο εἰς τὸν ἀγρὸν, καὶ μετεσκευασμένα πάντα καταλαβὼν καὶ παρ' ἑτέρῳ τὴν κτῆσιν, πάλιν ἧκεν εἰς ἄστυ διαπορούμενος· κᾀκεῖ δὲ εἰς τὴν ἑαυτοῦ εἰσιὼν οἰκίαν, περιέτυχε τοῖς πυνθανομένοις, τίς εἴη· ἕως τὸν νεώτερον ἀδελφὸν εὑρών, τότε ἤδη γέροντα ὄντα, πᾶσαν ἔμαθε παρ' ἐκείνου τὴν ἀλήθειαν. . . . καὶ ἐπανελθὼν ἐπ' οἴκου, μετ' οὐ πολὺ μετήλλαξεν, ὥς φησι Φλέγων ἐν τῷ περὶ μακροβίων, βιοὺς ἔτη ἑπτὰ καὶ πεντήκοντα καὶ ἑκατόν· ὡς δὲ Κρῆτες λέγουσι, ἑνὸς δέοντα τριακόσια· ὡς δὲ Ξενοφάνης ὁ Κολοφώνιος ἀκηκοέναι φησί, τέτταρα πρὸς τοῖς πεντήκοντα καὶ ἑκατόν* (Diog. Laertii, *De Vitis Philosophorum*, lib. I, cap. x. 2, 4). The tale has obtained a new lease of life in the New World under the form of Rip Van Winkle's somewhat similar adventure.

of that character. Muḥammad has, however, introduced into it another element of error, the source of which we must trace before entering upon the narrative itself.

In Sûrah XIX., Maryam, 28, 29, we are told that when Mary came to her people after the birth of our Lord, they said to her, "O Mary, truly thou hast done a strange thing. *O sister of Aaron*, thy father was not a man of wickedness, and thy mother was not rebellious." From these words it is evident that, in Muḥammad's opinion, Mary was identical with Miriam, the sister of Moses and Aaron[1]! This is made still more clear by Sûrah LVI., At Taḥrîm, 12, where Mary is styled "the daughter of 'Imrân," the latter being the Arabic form of Amram, who in the Pentateuch is called the father of "Aaron and Moses and Miriam *their sister*" (Num. xxvi. 59). The title "sister of Aaron" is given to Miriam in Exod. xv. 20, and it must be from this passage that Muḥammad borrowed the expression. The reason of the mistake which identifies the Mother of our Saviour with a woman who lived about one thousand five hundred and seventy years before His birth is evidently the fact that in Arabic both names, Mary and Miriam, are one and the same in form, *Maryam*.

[1] In the *Ṣaḥîḥ* of Muslim (*Kitâbu'l Âdâb*) we are told that the Christians of Najrân pointed this blunder out to Al Mughairah. He consulted Muḥammad about it, but could get no satisfactory answer.

The chronological difficulty of the identification does not seem to have occurred to Muḥammad. It puts us in mind of the tale in the Shâhnâmeh, where Firdausî tells us that, when the hero Farîdûn had defeated Ḍaḥḥâk (in Persian pronounced Ẓaḥḥâk), he found in the tyrant's castle two sisters of Jamshîd, who were kept in confinement there. Farîdûn was, we are told, smitten with their charms. This is an instance[1] of "bonus dormitat Homerus" on some one's part, for from other parts of the poem we learn that these fair damsels had remained in Ḍaḥḥâk's custody from the beginning of the latter's reign, nearly one thousand years before! Muḥammad's error, however, is chronologically far more serious even than this, which may be permissible in a romance but not in a "Revelation." Muḥammadan commentators have in vain attempted to disprove this charge of historical inaccuracy.

If it be necessary to adduce any other explanation of Muḥammad's blunder, it has been suggested[2] that it may be found in the Jewish tradition which asserts regarding Miriam that "The Angel of Death did not exercise dominion over her, but on the contrary she died with a (Divine) kiss, and worms and insects did not exercise dominion over her."

[1] But Firdausî is following the Avestâ here in telling us that Farîdûn (Avestic *Thraetaona*) married these women, Arnavâz and Shahrnâz (in Avestic Arenavâchî and Savanhavâchî); Yeshts, v. 34; ix. 14; xv. 24.

[2] R. Abraham Geiger, *Was hat Mohammed*, p. 172.

But, even so, the Jews never ventured to assert that Miriam remained alive until the time of Christ, nor to identify her with the Virgin Mary.

Let us now see what the Qur'ân and the Traditions relate regarding the latter.

In Sûrah III., Âl 'Imrân, 31, 32, we read:—

"When 'Imrân's wife said, 'My Lord, verily I have dedicated to Thee what is in my womb, as consecrated: receive it therefore from me: verily Thou art the Hearer, the Knower.' When therefore she bore her, she said, 'My Lord, verily I have borne her, a female'—and God was well aware of what she had borne, and the male is not as the female—'and verily I have named her Mary, and verily I commit her and her seed unto Thee from Satan the stoned.' Accordingly her Lord received her with fair acceptance, and He made her grow with fair growth, and Zacharias reared her. Whenever Zacharias entered the shrine unto her, he found food near her. He said, 'O Mary, whence is this to thee?' She said, 'It is from God: verily God feedeth whomsoever He willeth, without a reckoning.'"

In addition to and explanation of this narrative, Baiḍâwî and other commentators and traditionists inform us of the following particulars. 'Imrân's wife was barren and advanced in age. One day, on seeing a bird giving food to its young ones, she longed for offspring, and entreated that God would bestow on her a child. She said, "O my

God, if Thou givest me a child, whether it be a son or a daughter, I shall offer it as a gift in Thy presence in the Temple at Jerusalem." God heard and answered her prayer, and she conceived and bore a daughter, Mary. Jalâlu'ddîn tells us that the name of Mary's mother was Ḥannâ. When she brought Mary to the Temple and handed her over to the priests, they accepted the offering and appointed Zacharias to guard the child. He placed her in a room, and permitted no one but himself[1] to enter it; but an angel supplied her with her daily food.

Returning to the Qur'ân (Sûrah III., 37–42), we learn that, when Mary was older, "The angels said, 'O Mary, verily God hath chosen thee and purified thee, and He hath chosen thee above the women of the worlds. O Mary, be devout to thy Lord, and worship, and bow with those that bow.' That is part of the announcement of the invisible; we reveal it to thee[2]; and thou[2] wast not with them when they threw their reeds (to see) which of them should rear Mary: and thou[2] wast not with them when they disagreed. When the angels said, 'O Mary, verily God giveth thee good tidings of a Word from Himself, whose name is the Messiah, Jesus Son of Mary, illustrious in the world and in the hereafter, and from among those who draw

[1] A reference to the Law which prohibited any but the High Priest from entering the Holy of Holies.

[2] *i.e.* Muḥammad.

near (to God): and He shall speak to men in the cradle and when grown up, and He is of the Just ones,' she said, 'My Lord, whence shall I have a child, since no human being hath touched me?' He said, 'Thus God createth what He willeth: when He hath decreed a matter, then indeed He saith to it, Be!—therefore it exists.'"

In reference to what is said in these verses about "casting reeds" or *pens*, Baiḍâwî and Jalâlu'ddîn state that Zacharias and twenty-six other priests were rivals to one another in their desire to be Mary's guardian. They therefore went to the bank of the Jordan and threw their reeds into the water; but all the reeds sank except that of Zacharias, and on this account the latter was appointed her guardian.

Turning to Sûrah XIX., Maryam, 16–35, we find there the following narrative of the birth of Christ:

"And in the Book [1] do thou [2] mention Mary, when she retired from her family to an Eastern place. Then apart from them she assumed a veil. Then We sent unto her Our Spirit [3]: accordingly he showed himself to her as a well-formed human being. She said, 'Verily I take refuge in the Merciful One from thee, if thou art God-fearing.' He said, 'Truly I am a messenger of thy Lord that

[1] *i. e.* the Qur'ân (commentators). [2] *i. e.* Muḥammad.

[3] The angel Gabriel, who is hence called the Holy Spirit by Muslims.

I should give to thee a pure man-child.' She said, 'Whence shall I have a man-child, since no human being hath touched me, and I am not rebellious[1]?' He said, 'Thus hath thy Lord said, It is easy for Me, and let Us make Him a sign unto men and a mercy from us, and it is a thing decided.' Accordingly she conceived Him[2]: then she retired with him to a distant place. Then labour-pains brought her to the trunk of the palm-tree[3]. She said, 'O would that I had died ere this and had become forgotten, forgotten!' Thereupon he[4] called aloud to her from beneath her: 'Grieve thou not; thy Lord hath made a brook beneath thee. And do thou shake towards thyself the trunk of the palm-tree: it shall let fall upon thee freshly-gathered dates. Eat therefore and drink and brighten thy eye[5]; then, if thou seest any human being, then say, Verily I have vowed unto my Lord a fast, therefore I shall surely not speak to any man to-day.' Accordingly she brought Him[6] to her people, carrying Him. They said, 'O Mary, truly thou hast done a vile thing. O sister of Aaron, thy father was not a man of wickedness, and thy mother was not rebellious[7].' Then she made a sign unto Him[6]. They said,

[1] *Or*, unchaste. [2] Jesus.

[3] Note the definite article.

[4] Commentators are doubtful whether this is Jesus or Gabriel.

[5] That is, "Rejoice." The birth of a boy is still said to be a "brightening of the eyes" in the East, and congratulations are expressed by the formula in the text.

[6] The Child. [7] *Or*, unchaste.

'How shall we speak to one who is a child in the cradle?' He[1] said, 'Verily I am God's servant: He hath brought Me the Book[2] and hath made Me a Prophet. And He hath made Me blessed wherever I am, and hath prescribed for Me prayer and alms, as long as I live, and to be well-behaved to My mother, and He hath not made Me violent, wretched. And peace upon Me the day I was born, and the day I shall die, and the day I shall be raised up alive.' That is Jesus, Son of Mary; a statement of the truth, concerning which they doubt."

We can trace every single matter here mentioned to some apocryphal source, as will be evident from the passages which we now proceed to adduce.

In the *Protevangelium of James the Less*[3], in reference to Mary's birth, we read:

"And having gazed fixedly into the sky Anna[4] saw a nest of sparrows in the bay-tree, and she made lamentation in herself, saying, 'Woe is me! woe is me! who hath begotten me? . . . Woe is me! to what am I likened? I am not likened to the birds of the air, for even the birds of the air are productive in thy sight, O Lord.' . . . And lo! an angel of the Lord stood by, saying unto her, 'Anna! Anna! the Lord God hath hearkened unto thy petition; thou shalt conceive and shalt bear,

[1] Jesus. [2] The Gospel.

[3] *Protevangelium Iacobi Minoris*, capp. 3, 4, 5.

[4] So in Muḥammadan Tradition, as we have seen, Mary's mother is named Ḥannà.

and thy seed shall be spoken of in all the world.' But Anna said, 'As the Lord my God liveth, if I bear either male or female, I shall offer it as a gift unto the Lord my God, and it shall continue to do Him service all the days of its life.' . . . But her months were fulfilled, and in the ninth month Anna brought forth. . . . And she gave breast to the child and called her Mary."

The tale then proceeds to tell how, when the child was old enough to leave her mother, she was taken to the Temple at Jerusalem by Anna, according to her vow. It then continues:—

"The[1] priest accepted her and kissed and blessed her and said, 'The Lord God hath magnified thy name amid all the generations of the earth: upon thee at the end of the days shall the Lord God manifest the redemption of the Children of Israel.' . . . But Mary was like a dove reared in the Lord's shrine (ἐν τῷ ναῷ Κυρίου), and she was wont to receive food from an angel's hand. But when she became twelve years of age, there was held a council of the priests, who said, 'Lo! Mary hath become twelve years old in the shrine of the Lord, what therefore are we to do with her?' . . . And lo! an angel of the Lord stood by him, saying, 'Zacharias! Zacharias! go forth and call together the widowers of the people, and let them bring each a rod, and to whomsoever the Lord God shall show a sign, his wife shall she be.' And the heralds

[1] *Op. cit.*, capp. 7, 8, 9, 11.

went forth throughout all the coast of Judaea, and the trumpet of the Lord sounded, and they all ran. But Joseph, casting away his adze, himself ran also into the synagogue: and having been assembled they went away unto the priest. And the priest took the rods of all, and went into the Temple and prayed. But having ended his prayer he came forth and gave to each one his rod, and there was no sign in them. But Joseph received the last rod. And lo! a dove came forth from the rod and flew up upon Joseph's head. And the priest said unto him, 'Thou hast obtained by lot to receive the virgin of the Lord: receive her unto thyself to guard.' . . . And Joseph, being affrighted, received her to guard. . . . But Mary, having taken a pitcher, went out to fill it with water. And lo! a voice, saying, 'Hail, O highly favoured! the Lord is with thee: blessed art thou among women.' And she looked around to right and left [to see] whence this voice came. And having become alarmed she departed unto her house; and having set down the pitcher . . . she sat down upon the seat. . . . And lo! an angel of the Lord stood by, saying unto her, 'Fear not, Mary, for thou hast found favour in God's sight, and thou shalt conceive from His Word (ἐκ λόγου αὐτοῦ).' But Mary having heard considered in herself, saying, 'Shall I conceive according as every woman beareth?' And the angel saith unto her, 'Not thus, Mary; for the power of the Highest shall overshadow thee, therefore also the holy thing that is to be born shall be called Son of the Highest: and thou shalt call His name Jesus."

The legend of Mary's being brought up in the Temple is found in many other apocryphal works besides the one we have here quoted. For example, in the Coptic "History of the Virgin[1]" we read:—

"She was nourished in the Temple like the doves, and food was brought to her from the heavens by the angels of God. And she was wont to do service in the Temple; the angels of God used to minister unto her. But they used often to bring her fruits also from the Tree of Life, that she might eat of them with joy." And in another Coptic work entitled the "Story of the Decease of Joseph[2]" the following passage occurs:—"Mary used to dwell in the Temple and worship there with holiness, and she grew up until she became twelve years old. In her parents' house she abode three years, and in the Temple of the Lord nine years more. Then the priests, when they perceived that that virgin lived chastely and dwelt in the fear of the Lord, spake to one another, saying, 'Let us seek out a good man and betroth her unto him until the time of the marriage-feast. . . . And they forthwith summoned the tribe of Judah and chose out from it twelve men according to the names of

[1] *Coptic Apocryphal Gospels*, p. 15: Frag. ii. A: lines 10–12.

[2] *Op. cit.*, capp. 3, 4, p. 132.

the twelve tribes of Israel. The lot fell upon that good old man, Joseph."

Returning now to the *Protevangelium*, we are told that, when the fact became known that Mary had conceived, Joseph and she were brought before the priests for judgment. The story then goes on:—

"And [1] the priest said, 'Mary, why hast thou done this and hast humbled thy soul? Thou hast forgotten the Lord thy God, thou who wast brought up in the Holy of Holies and didst receive food at an angel's hand, and didst hear the hymns ... Why hast thou done this?' But she wept bitterly, saying, 'As the Lord God liveth, I am pure in His sight, and I know not a man.'"

Afterwards we are informed that Joseph and Mary went from Nazareth to Bethlehem. Failing to find room in the caravansarai at the latter place, they went to abide in a cave, and there the Lord Jesus was born. The words of the original, omitting as usual everything not connected with our present purpose, may be thus translated:—

"And [2] he found a cave and led her in ... But [3] I,

[1] *Protevangelium Iacobi Minoris*, cap. 15.

[2] *Op. cit.*, cap. 18.

[3] The scene here described is not mentioned in the Qur'ân itself, nor do Muḥammadan traditions clearly record it in reference to the birth of Christ. It is upon this description that Milton dwells in his Ode "On the Morning of Christ's Nativity":

Joseph, . . . looked up into the heaven and saw the vault of the heaven stationary[1] and the birds of the air trembling. And I looked upon the earth, and saw a dish laid out and workmen seated (ἀνακειμένους), and their hands were in the dish, and those who were raising [the food to their lips] did not raise it, and those who were putting it into their mouths did not put it in, but the faces of them all were looking upwards. And I saw sheep being driven, and the sheep stood still; but the shepherd

"No war, or battle's sound
Was heard the world around:
The idle spear and shield were high up hung,
The hooked chariot stood
Unstained with hostile blood,
The trumpet spake not to the armed throng.
. . . .
But peaceful was the night
Wherein the Prince of Light
His reign of peace upon the earth began:
. . . .
While birds of calm sit brooding on the charmed wave.
The stars, with deep amaze,
Stand fixed in steadfast gaze. . . ."

But something of the same thing has left its trace upon later Muḥammadan legend, only in reference to *Muḥammad's* birth. Thus in the *Rauḍatu'l Aḥbâb*, Fâṭimah, daughter of 'Abdu'llâh, is reported as having said: "I was with Âminah" (Muḥammad's mother) "when the symptoms of her approaching confinement set in: and, on looking up to heaven, I saw the stars to such an extent incline towards the earth that I thought they must fall down." Or, according to another account, "The stars were so near the earth that I thought they would fall upon my head." (Quoted by Dr. Koelle, *Mohammed and Mohammedanism*, p. 257.)

[1] Cf. Plautus, *Amphitruo*, Act I., Sc. i., vv. 115–20.

raised [his crook] to smite them, and his hand remained aloft. And I looked to the torrent and saw kids, and their mouths were applied to the water and not drinking, and all things astounded."

The incident of Mary and the palm-tree as related above (Sûrah XIX, Maryam, 23–6) is apparently taken from the apocryphal work entitled "History of the Nativity of Mary and the Infancy of the Saviour," although, as we shall see, we can trace both accounts to a probably more ancient source. In the book to which we have just referred, the event is connected with the Flight into Egypt. The tale records how the Holy Family started on the journey and for two days travelled on quietly. It then continues:—

"But[1] on the third day after he had set out, it came to pass that Mary became exhausted in the desert through the excessive heat of the sun. When therefore she saw a tree, she said unto Joseph, 'Let us rest a little while under the shadow of this tree.' And Joseph hasted and brought her to that palm-tree, and took her down off her beast. When Mary sat down, she looked up to the top of the palm-tree, and seeing it full of fruit said to Joseph, 'I desire, if it be possible, to take of the fruit of this palm-tree.' And Joseph said unto her, 'I marvel that thou speakest thus, since thou seest how high the branches of this palm-tree are. But

[1] *Hist. Nativitat. Mariae*, cap. 20.

I am extremely anxious about water, for it has now been exhausted in our skin-bottles, and we have nowhere whence we can fill them and quench our thirst.' Then the Child Jesus, who with a joyful countenance lay in His mother the Virgin Mary's bosom, said to the palm-tree, 'O tree, lower thy branches and refresh My mother with thy fruit.' Instantly the palm-tree at this word bowed its head to the sole of Mary's feet: and they all plucked the fruit which it bore, and were refreshed. And afterwards, when all its fruit had been plucked, the tree still remained bent, since it was waiting to rise up at the command of Him, by whose command it had bowed down. Then Jesus said unto it, 'O palm-tree, arise and be of good cheer, and be thou a companion of My trees that are in My Father's Paradise. But with thy roots open the spring that is hidden in the ground, and let water flow forth from that spring to quench our thirst.' And the palm-tree instantly stood erect, and streams of very clear, cool, and very sweet water began to come forth from amid its roots. And when they beheld those streams of water, they rejoiced with exceeding great joy; and they with all their quadrupeds and attendants were satisfied and thanked God."

Instead of connecting the palm-tree and the stream that flowed from beneath it with the account of the Flight into Egypt, the Qur'ân, as we have seen, connects them very closely with the birth of Christ, representing Him as having been born at the foot of the tree, and at that moment (according to one explanation) directing the tree to let its fruit fall for Mary to eat, and telling her of the flowing streamlet. From its accordance with this apocryphal Gospel in this respect, it is evident that this explanation of the words of the Qur'ân is more likely to be correct than the gloss which attributes the speech to Gabriel.

But we have now to inquire from what source the Qur'ân borrowed the idea that Christ was born at the foot of a tree: and also what is the origin of the legend that the tree bowed down to let the mother and Child eat of its fruit. It is hardly necessary to say that for neither the one statement nor the other is there the very slightest foundation in the Canonical Gospels.

The source of both incidents is found in the books of the Buddhist Pâlî Canon, which, as we are informed in the *Mahâ-Vaṃso*, was reduced to writing in the reign of King Vaṭṭâgâmani of Ceylon, probably about 80 B.C. at latest[1]. But it is very possible that very considerable parts of these Pâlî books were composed several hundred years earlier. The legends contained in them were, in later but still very early times, widely spread, not only in India and Ceylon but also in Central Asia, China, Tibet, and other lands. Buddhist missionaries are mentioned in Yesht XIII., 16,

[1] Vide *The Noble Eightfold Path*, pp. 69, 70.

as having appeared in Persia as early as the second century before Christ. The influence which Buddhism exercised on thought throughout Western, as well as Central, Eastern and Southern, Asia was immense. Manichaism, Gnosticism and other heresies were largely due to this, as was the rise of Monasticism[1]. Several passages in the apocryphal Gospels show that ideas of Buddhist origin had gained access to the minds of the writers of these spurious works, though doubtless these men were quite unaware of the real source of their inspiration. It was easy for Muḥammad therefore to be misled in the same way; and we can point to the very passages in the Pâlî books which represent the earliest known form of the legends about the tree.

One of these occurs in the *Nidânakathâ Jâtakaṃ* (cap. i., pp. 50–3). There we are told that when Mâyâ, who was to be the mother of Gotamo Buddha, was with child and knew that her time was at hand, she obtained her husband Suddhodano's permission to return to her father's house to be delivered, according to the custom of the country. On the journey she and her handmaidens entered a beautiful forest, and Princess Mâyâ greatly admired the abundant flowers which she saw on some of the trees. In the words of the passage to which we refer, the account of what then took place runs thus:—

[1] *Op. cit.*, pp. 196 sqq.

"She[1], having gone to the foot of a well-omened *Sâl*-tree, became desirous of grasping a branch of the *Sâl*-tree. The *Sâl*-tree branch, having bent down like the end of a stick well softened with steam, came within the reach of the princess's hand. She, having stretched out her hand, seized the branch.... Childbirth came upon her just as she stood, grasping the branch of the *Sâl*-tree."

The differences between this and the account of Christ's birth as related in the passage in the Qur'ân which we have quoted above are but slight. Muḥammad mentions a palm-tree, the best-known of all trees to an Arab, in place of the species of flowering tree mentioned in the Buddhist book, since the *Sâl*-tree of India does not grow in Arabia. Doubtless the legend had changed in this way in its transmission, as is generally the case in similar tales. The Indian legend intimates that the exertion made by Buddha's mother in reaching after the flowers growing on the branch above her head brought on the child's birth unexpectedly. The Qur'ân seems to give no such good reason at all for the birth occurring below the palm-tree. But the stories are evidently one and the same. We notice here, as in the Qur'ân, that the tree bent down its

[1] "Sà mañgalasâlamûlaṃ gantvâ sâlasâkhâyaṃ gaṇhitukâmâ ahosi. Sâlasâkhâ suseditavettagaṃ viya oṇamitvâ deviyâ hatthapathaṃ upagañchi. Sâ hatthaṃ pasâretvâ sâkhaṃ aggahesi.... Sâlasâkhaṃ gahetvâ tiṭṭhamânâya eva c' assâ gabbhavuṭṭhânaṃ ahosi."

branches to let Mâyâ pluck the flowers,—or, as the Qur'ân has it, let its ripe dates fall upon Mary.

The other account of this latter incident,—that given in the apocryphal Gospel,—is connected with the Flight into Egypt, when our Lord was an infant. This is parallel with what we read in the Cariyâ-Piṭakaṃ (cap. i., poem ix.). There we are informed that in a former birth Buddha was a prince called Vessantaro. Having offended his people, he was banished from his kingdom, along with his wife and two little children. As they wandered towards the distant mountains, where they wished to find an asylum, the children became hungry. Then, the Buddhist narrative tells us:—

"If [1] the children see fruit-bearing trees on the mountain-side, the children weep for their fruit. Having seen the children weeping, the great, lofty

[1] Verses 34, 35:—

"Yadi passanti pavane dârikâ phalite dume,
tesaṃ phalânaṃ hetumhi uparodanti dârikâ.
Rodante dârike disvâ ubbidhâ vipulâ dumâ,
Sayam ev' oṇamitvâna upagacchanti dârike."

The story of Buddha's birth under a tree is also found in the *Romantic History of Buddha*, translated by Beal from the Chinese Sanskrit (p. 43), and also in the *Phû-yau-king* (ibid., p. 347).

The fancy that Mary was brought up in the Temple is, of course, along with the name of her mother Anna (Hannah), derived from the account of Samuel's dedication by his mother Hannah. But it is an evidence of great ignorance to imagine the same thing possible in the case of a *girl*, and still more so to say, as the apocryphal books do, that Mary was brought up in the *Holy of Holies*!

trees, having even of themselves bowed down, approach the children."

It is clear that both the Qur'ân and the author of the apocryphal "History of the Nativity of Mary" have unconsciously borrowed from Buddhist sources these particular incidents. This fact of course disproves the truth of the narrative.

Were proof required to show that, even as late as Muḥammad's time, Buddhist legends were prevalent in Western Asia and were accepted as Christian history, it would be afforded by the existence of the tale of "Barlaam and Josaphat." This legend was written in Greek in the sixth century of the Christian era, as some hold, though it is more generally attributed to Johannes Damascenus, who flourished at the court of the Khalîfah Al Manṣûr (A.D. 753–74). Josaphat, the Christian prince of the book, is undoubtedly Buddha himself, and his name is a corruption of *Bodhisattva*, one of Buddha's many titles. The main source of the tale is the Sanskṛit legendary story of Buddha known as the *Lalita Vistara.* Yet Josaphat is a saint in both the Greek and the Roman Churches, in the former of which August 26 is sacred to him, in the latter November 27.

3. *Story of the Childhood of Jesus.*

In what has been already related we have learnt something of what the Qur'ân teaches on this subject. But we must now deal with the matter more at length.

In Sûrah III., Âl 'Imrân, 41, 43, we are informed that before Christ's birth the Angel said of Him:—"And He shall speak to men in the cradle" . . . And in Sûrah XIX., Maryam, 29–31, as we have already seen, we are informed that, when the Virgin Mary's people reproached her, she made a sign towards the Child, implying that they should ask Him of His origin. They said in surprise, "How shall we talk with one who is a child in the cradle?" Then the Child Jesus spoke to them, saying, "Verily I am God's Servant: He hath brought Me the Book and made Me a Prophet."

The origin of this legend is not far to seek. We have already seen that one of the apocryphal Gospels represents Christ, when on His journey to Egypt in His infancy, as addressing the palm-tree and bidding it bow down and permit His Mother to pluck its fruit. But probably the source from which Muḥammad borrowed the incident is the *Injîlu 't Ṭufûliyyah*, better known as the Arabic Gospel of the Infancy. In the first chapter of that work we read:—

"We have found it recorded in the book of Josephus the Chief Priest, who was in the time of Christ (and men say that he was Caiaphas), that this man said that Jesus spake when He was in the cradle, and said to Mary His Mother, 'Verily I am Jesus, the Son of God, the Word which thou hast borne, according as the angel Gabriel gave thee the good news; and My Father hath sent Me for the salvation of the world.'"

Of course Muḥammad could not represent Christ as using the words which this apocryphal Gospel attributes to Him, for in the Qur'ân the Divine Sonship of Christ is everywhere denied. Therefore, while believing and stating that Jesus spoke when an infant in the cradle, Muḥammad in his account has put into His mouth words which seemed to him more suitable and more consonant with Islâm. Otherwise the story is the same.

The style of the Arabic of this apocryphal Gospel, however, is so bad that it is hardly possible to believe that it dates from Muḥammad's time. As, however, Arabic has never been supposed to be the language in which the work was composed, this is a matter of little or no consequence. From a study of the book there seems little room for doubt that it has been translated into Arabic from the Coptic, in which language it may have been composed. This explains in what way Muḥammad most probably became acquainted with the legend. For it is a well-known fact that the Christian governor of Egypt sent him a present of two Coptic girls, one of whom, "Mary the Copt," became one of his favourite concubines. This girl, though not well acquainted with the Gospel, must doubtless have known so popular a legend as that contained in the "Gospel of the Infancy" at that time was. Muḥammad probably learnt the tale from her, and, fancying it to be contained in the Gospels universally accepted by Christians as of Divine authority, he on that account incorporated it into the Qur'ân. Of course it is possible that he had others besides Mary who told him Coptic legends, but, whoever his informant or informants may have been, it is clear that the source of the story of the miracle is the one we have mentioned.

Now the Arabic "Gospel of the Infancy" is one of a number of apocryphal works of late or of uncertain date, which were never by any Christian sect regarded as inspired. Others of the same class which have left their mark upon the Qur'ân are the "Gospel of Thomas the Israelite," the "Protevangelium of James," the "Gospel of Nicodemus" (otherwise called the "Gesta Pilati"), and the "Narrative of Joseph of Arimathaea." Muḥammad, as has been already observed, seems to have had a peculiar gift for discovering unreliable sources of information, for he never appears to quote one which is merely of doubtful authority. These books and others like them, though very popular among ignorant Christians then and even in later times, can hardly be said to have been intended to impose on any one, they are so manifestly religious romances. They dealt with matters concerning which much curiosity was very naturally felt, and were therefore welcomed by men who did not care to inquire whether what they read was true or false. They were quite contented to believe that these stories were old traditions and dealt with subjects on which the canonical books gave little or no information. No doubt some persons gave credit to these legends, but no man of any learning can be mentioned who did so in the case of any one of the books we have named. They were not even deemed of sufficient importance to be included among the *Antilegomena*. Some of them may have been reconstructed on the basis of earlier works that have perished, though with the addition of many fabulous elements. But whether this be so or not, they are sometimes found to incorporate legends of considerable antiquity, if of no authority. We have seen instances in which certain stories can be traced to very ancient Buddhist fables. The tale of Jesus speaking to men when He was still an infant in the cradle is another example of somewhat the same kind, though it cannot be traced back to the Pâlî Canon. The same tale is told of Buddha in the *Lalita Vistara*, in the *Buddha-Carita* [1], and in other Sanskṛit works. In the "Romantic Legend [2]" we are gravely informed that, as soon as he was born, Buddha "forthwith walked seven steps towards each quarter of the horizon; and, as he walked, at each step there sprang from the earth beneath his feet a lotus flower; and, as he looked steadfastly in each direction, his mouth uttered these words,

[1] Book I. § 34, ed. Cowell.

[2] Beal, *Rom. Legend*, p. 44.

. . . 'In all the world I am the very chief.'" In another[1] Chinese Sanskṛit work the same story is told, with this difference that Buddha's words are there said to have been, "This birth is in the condition of a Buddha: after this I have done with renewed birth: now only am I born this once, *for the purpose of saving all the world.*" It will be noticed that, making allowance for the difference between the non-theistic Buddhist system and the Christian one, this last quotation bears a considerable resemblance to the words attributed to the infant Christ in our quotation from the Arabic "Gospel of the Infancy": in fact the concluding words of the latter are almost a verbal translation of the former[2].

The supposed fact that our Lord spoke in His

[1] Beal's version of the *Fo-sho-hing-tsan-king* (pp. 3, 4).

[2] In the Zamyâd Yesht of the Zoroastrians a somewhat similar account of speaking at birth is mentioned in connexion with the monster Snâvidhka, who when still very young said: 'I am still an infant, and I am not yet grown up: if I ever do grow up I shall make the earth a wheel, I shall make the heavens a chariot: I shall bring down the Good Spirit from the bright Garô-nmânem" [the highest heaven, the abode of Ahurô Mazdâo, corresponding to the Muḥammadan '*Arsh*]: "I shall cause the Evil Spirit to rush up from miserable hell. They will bear my chariot, both the Good Spirit and the Evil Spirit, unless the manly-hearted Keresâspa slay me." The mention of the "wheel" and the "chariot" in this passage distinctly indicates Buddhist influence in Persia, and reminds us of how Buddha was said to have "turned the wheel of the Law," implying his claim to universal dominịon. Hence the idea of the infant speaking at birth also is seen to be not an original Zoroastrian but a Buddhist legend.

cradle is also asserted in the following passage from Sûrah V., Al Mâidah, 109, 110, together with other matters which we shall now consider. For convenience' sake we quote both verses in full:—

"When God said, 'O Jesus, Son of Mary, remember My favour towards Thee and towards Thy mother, when I strengthened Thee with the Holy Spirit; Thou dost speak unto men in the cradle and as an adult: and when I taught Thee the Book and wisdom and the Law and the Gospel; and when Thou dost create from clay as it were the figure of a bird by My permission, then Thou dost breathe into it, thereupon it becometh a bird by My permission; and Thou dost cleanse the blind and the leper by My permission; and when Thou dost bring forth the dead by My permission; and when I restrained the Children of Israel from Thee, when Thou didst come to them with the evident signs: therefore those of them who disbelieved said, This is nothing except evident magic.'"

What is here related of our Lord's miracles of healing the blind, cleansing the leper and raising the dead, may be derived indirectly from the four canonical Gospels, though similar events are not excluded—as they could not well be—from the apocryphal Gospels. But the point of importance for our present purpose is what is said about His creating a bird out of clay and giving it life. This incident is derived from the apocryphal "Gospel of Thomas the Israelite," in the second chapter of which we read:—

"This child, Jesus, having become five years old, was playing at the crossing of a brook, and He had collected together into pools the running waters and was making them clean forthwith, and with a single word did He command them. And having made some clay fine, He formed out of it twelve sparrows. And it was the Sabbath when He did these things. There were, however, many other children also playing with Him. But a certain Jew, having seen what Jesus was doing, that He was playing on the Sabbath day, went away immediately and told His father Joseph, 'Lo! thy child is at the brook, and having taken clay He hath formed twelve little birds out of it, and He hath profaned the Sabbath.' And Joseph, having come to the spot and having seen, cried out to Him, saying, 'Why dost Thou on the Sabbath do these things which it is not lawful to do?' But Jesus, having clapped His hands together, cried out to the sparrows and said to them, 'Go!' And the sparrows, having taken flight, departed twittering. But the Jews, having seen this, were astounded; and having gone away they related to their chief men what they saw that Jesus did."

It is worthy of note that the whole of this fable occurs twice over in the Arabic "Gospel of the Infancy," in chapter xxxvi, and again in another form in chapter xlvi. The reason of this is that the latter part of the book is taken from the "Gospel of Thomas the Israelite."

We notice here again that, while the legend is evidently the same as that briefly referred to in the Qur'ân, yet the difference is sufficient to prove that Muḥammad was reproducing a shortened form of it from memory, and was not consulting any written document. Hence he mentions only one bird instead of twelve, and speaks of life being given to it by the breath of Jesus and not by a command of His. The brief reference made to the tale in the Qur'ân shows that the story had obtained wide currency and was generally believed at the time. This again proves how little knowledge of the New Testament there then was in Medina; for not only are no such accounts of miracles performed by our Saviour in His childhood recorded in the canonical Gospels, but John ii. 11 shows that none were wrought until after His Baptism at the age of about thirty.

4. *Story of the Table.*

This supposed miracle of Christ is related in Sûrah V., Al Mâidah, 112–15, and gives its name[1] to that Sûrah. Translated as literally as possible, the tale runs thus:—

"When the Apostles[2] said, 'O Jesus, Son of

[1] *Mâidah* means a table provided with food.

[2] The word used here (حواريّون) is always applied to the

Mary, can Thy Lord cause a Table to descend upon us from the heaven?' He said, "Fear ye God, if ye be believers.' They said, 'We desire to eat from it and that our hearts be confirmed, and that we may know that Thou hast told us truth and may be witnesses unto it[1].' Jesus, Son of Mary, said, 'O God, our Lord, cause a table to descend unto us from the heaven which shall be a festival[2] unto us, to the first of us and to the last of us[2], and a sign from Thee, and feed Thou us: and Thou art the best of feeders.' God said, 'Verily I cause it to descend unto you: but whosoever among you thereafter shall disbelieve, I shall assuredly punish him with a punishment wherewith I shall not punish any other creature.'"

Unless there be some Æthiopian legend on the subject which the early Muslim refugees had brought back with them from that country, we must trace this myth to a misunderstanding of certain passages in the New Testament. If there be some such legend found elsewhere, which we have not traced, it must have had the same ultimate source. One of the New Testament passages which doubtless helped to give rise to it is the verse

Apostles of Christ exclusively. It is an Æthiopic word. Does this show any connexion between the fable and some legend current in Æthiopia, whither Muḥammad's first converts fled for refuge?

[1] To the Table.

[2] These expressions show that there is a reference to the institution of the Lord's Supper.

M

(Luke xx. 30) in which our Lord says to His disciples, "That ye may eat and drink *at My Table* in My kingdom." Muḥammad doubtless knew that the Christians celebrated the Lord's Supper, in accordance with Matt. xxvi. 20–9; Mark xiv. 17–25; Luke xxii. 14–30; John xiii. 1–30; and 1 Cor. xi. 20–34. But what doubtless led to the idea that the Table descended from Heaven was the passage in the Acts of the Apostles (x. 9–16), in which we read the following account of Peter's vision:—

"Peter went up upon the housetop to pray, about the sixth hour: and he became hungry, and *desired to eat*: but while they made ready, he fell into a trance; and he beholdeth *the heaven opened, and a certain vessel descending, as it were a great sheet, let down by four corners upon the earth*: wherein were all manner of fourfooted beasts and creeping things of the earth and fowls of the heaven. *And there came a voice to him*, 'Rise, Peter; kill and *eat*.' But Peter said, 'Not so, Lord; for I have never eaten anything that is common or unclean.' And a voice came unto him again the second time, 'What God hath cleansed, make not thou common.' And this was done thrice: and straightway the vessel was received up into heaven."

The concluding words of the passage which we have quoted from Sûrah Al Mâidah are an additional proof that Muḥammad was thinking of the Lord's Supper, for they seem to be a faint echo of

St. Paul's warning against unworthily partaking of that sacrament (1 Cor. xi. 27–9).

The whole passage is an additional proof of how very little knowledge of the New Testament Muḥammad had. No one who had read the book or heard it read could have confounded Peter's vision with the institution of the Lord's Supper, or transformed that vision into the descent of a table of provisions from heaven in our Lord's lifetime. The passage is an interesting illustration of the way in which legends grow.

5. *Muḥammad's Misconception of the Doctrine of the Trinity.*

In the early part of the present chapter we have briefly referred to this subject, but it must be again noticed here to make our treatment of the influence of "Christian" ideas and practices upon Islâm somewhat more complete. The conception which Muḥammad formed of the Christian doctrine of the Trinity in Unity is about as accurate as that which the last few paragraphs show that he entertained with reference to the institution of the Lord's Supper. This is evident from the following passages:—

Sûrah V., Al Mâidah, 116: "And when God said, 'O Jesus, Son of Mary, hast Thou said unto men, Take Me and My Mother as two gods besides God?'"

Sûrah IV., An Nisâ, 169: "O People of the Book,

be not extravagant in your religion, and do not say concerning God other than the truth. Truly the Messiah, Jesus, Son of Mary, is the Apostle of God and His Word which He cast into Mary, and a Spirit from Him. Therefore believe ye in God and His apostle, and say not 'Three.' Cease! it is well for you! Truly God is One God. Far be it from Him that He should have a Son. To Him belongs whatever is in the Heavens and whatever is in the Earth: and it sufficeth with God as a guardian."

Sûrah V., Al Mâidah, 77: 'They have indeed blasphemed who have said, 'Verily God is the Third of Three'; and there is no God but one God; and if they cease not from what they say, there shall surely touch those of them who have blasphemed a severe punishment."

These verses are explained by the commentators Jalâlu'ddîn and Yaḥyâ' as being the answer to the statement which Muḥammad heard certain Christians make that there are three Gods, that is to say God the Father, Mary, and Jesus. It is perfectly plain from these verses that Muḥammad really did believe that the Christian doctrine inculcated belief in three separate Divine Persons, Jesus and Mary being two of them. But our third quotation implies that Muḥammad—probably from what he had seen of "Christian" worship—thought that the order was Jesus, Mary, God, or Mary, Jesus, God. No reasonable man will wonder at the indignation with which Muḥammad in God's name abjures such blasphemy. We must all feel regret that the idolatrous worship offered to Mary led Muḥammad to believe that people who called her "Queen of Heaven" and "Mother of God" really attributed to her Divine attributes. He rightly perceived that God was practically dethroned in her favour. Had he been taught that the doctrine of the Unity of God is the very foundation of the Christian faith (Deut. vi. 4; Mark xii. 29), he might have become a Christian reformer. He can never have heard the true explanation of the Doctrine of the Trinity in Unity, otherwise he would have learnt that Christian theologians spoke of the Father not as "the Third of Three" but as the Πηγὴ[1] τῆς Θεότητος, the very "Fount of Deity."

It should be noticed, however, that, though the undue exaltation of the Virgin Mary, which led Muḥammad astray as to the true doctrine of the Bible, is contrary to the Christian faith, yet such false ideas and practices are distinctly encouraged by the teaching of many of the later apocryphal Gospels, particularly by those which formed the ultimate sources of Muḥammad's knowledge of Christianity. We mention this to prevent the possibility of any Muḥammadan reader supposing that he can find a way out of his difficulty by endeavouring to prove that such books as "The

[1] Cf. Athanasius, *Contra Arianos*, iv. 1, Λεχθείη δ' ἂν καὶ οὕτω "μία ἀρχὴ θεότητος," καὶ οὐ δύο ἀρχαί.

Nativity of Mary," "The Protevangelium of James the Less," and the Arabic "Gospel of the Infancy" are more authentic monuments of the early Christian faith as taught by Christ than are the canonical books of the New Testament! Experience of the Muḥammadan controversy renders the warning permissible.

6. *Denial of the Crucifixion of Christ.*

It is well known that all Muḥammadans have from the earliest times denied that Christ died on the Cross. In this they are supported by the Qur'ân, which, in Sûrah IV., An Nisâ, 156, represents the Jews as saying, "Verily we have slain the Messiah, Jesus, son of Mary, the Apostle of God." Muḥammad then in reply to them says, "And they slew Him not, and they crucified Him not, but He was represented unto them [by another] . . . And they slew Him not really, but on the contrary God exalted Him unto Himself."

Muḥammad's denial of the death of Christ on the Cross cannot be traced even to such untrustworthy authority as his favourite apocryphal Gospels. It is needless to say that he contradicts both the Old Testament Prophets and the New Testament Apostles, though doubtless merely through ignorance. It seemed to him to be derogatory to the dignity of Christ to have been crucified and put to death by His enemies; and Muḥammad was all the more convinced of this when he found his own enemies, the Jews, exulting at having slain Jesus. Hence he gladly adopted the assertion of certain heresiarchs, with whose views in other respects he had little in common. Several of these had, long before Muḥammad's time, denied the actual suffering of Christ. Irenaeus tells us with reference to the teaching of the Gnostic heretic Basilides, who flourished about A. D. 120, that, in speaking of Jesus, he taught his deluded followers "That[1] He had not suffered; and that a certain Simon of Cyrene had been compelled to carry His cross for Him; and that this man was crucified through ignorance and error, having been changed in form by Him, so that it should be thought that he was Jesus Himself." This language coincides very closely with that of the Qur'ân in this matter. Yet Muḥammad would have repudiated the principle upon which this view, according to Irenaeus, was based: for Basilides held that Jesus was identical with νοῦς or Mind, the first[2] emanation from the unknown God, and that He could not suffer because He had no real human body. This is absolutely opposed

[1] "Neque passum eum; et Simonem quendam Cyrenaeum angariatum portasse crucem eius pro eo; et hunc secundum ignorantiam et errorem crucifixum, transfiguratum ab eo, uti putaretur ipse esse Iesus."

[2] For our present purpose it is unnecessary to refer to the difference between Irenaeus' account and that given by Hippolytus in his *Philosophumena*. Much as the two reports differ in certain respects, they agree sufficiently in showing the general fact of Basilides' Gnostic views in those matters.

to the Qur'ân, which asserts that Jesus, though a Prophet and Apostle, was a merely human person, possessed of a human body, born of a human mother, and destined to die at some time or other. We see therefore that Muḥammad opposed the principle from which Basilides deduced a certain result, and yet accepted that result and recorded it in the Qur'ân. This is such an utterly illogical proceeding that it cannot be attributed to anything but a very natural ignorance.

But this view regarding Christ's dying only in appearance and not in reality was not confined to Basilides. Photius (820–91 *circa*) in his *Bibliotheca* (Cod. 114) mentions the fact that in an apocryphal book called the "Travels[1] of the Apostles" it was asserted "that Christ had not been crucified, but another in His stead." Manes or Mânî, the celebrated false prophet who at one time obtained so much influence in Persia, in a similar way held that "The[2] prince of darkness therefore was

[1] Περίοδοι Ἀποστόλων (quoted by Rodwell, *Koran*, p. 471, note): καὶ τὸν Χριστὸν μὴ σταυρωθῆναι, ἀλλ' ἕτερον ἀντ' αὐτοῦ.

[2] Manes, *Ep. Fund.*, *ap. Evodium*: "Princeps itaque tenebrarum cruci est affixus, idemque coronam spineam portavit." It is unnecessary here to appeal to the statement in the "Gospel of Barnabas" that Judas was crucified instead of Christ, as that work was written long after Muḥammad's time. The various and somewhat contradictory Traditions of the Muslims regarding the question whether Christ died or not; if so, how long He remained dead, and who was crucified in His place, will be found treated of in my *Religion of the Crescent*, Appendix A.

fastened to the cross, and the same person bore the crown of thorns." It cannot be said that Muḥammad denies Christ's death on good authority, or that in doing so he is in good company.

Yet in several places in the Qur'ân mention is made of the fact that Jesus was to die, like the rest of mankind. For example, in Sûrah III., Âl 'Imrân, 48, it is written:—

"When God said, 'O Jesus, verily it is I that cause Thee to expire and that exalt Thee unto Myself and purify Thee from those that have disbelieved.'"

So also in Sûrah XIX., Maryam, 34, Jesus in the cradle is represented as saying:—

"And peace upon Me the day I was born and the day I shall die and the day I shall be raised up alive."

Commentators are not perfectly agreed as to the exact meaning of these passages. Some hold that, when the Jews wished to crucify Christ, they seized and imprisoned Him and His Apostles on the evening preceding the Paschal feast, intending to slay Him the next morning. But in the night God sent Him the message, "Thou must through Me undergo death, but immediately afterwards Thou shalt be taken up to Me and freed from the power of the unbelievers." Accordingly Jesus expired and remained dead for three hours. Others mention a longer period. Finally, however, Gabriel appeared and carried Him off through the window and up to heaven, without this being perceived by anyone. An unbelieving Jewish spy was mistaken for Him and crucified in His stead[1]. But the more common, in fact the all but universal opinion of Muslims at the present day, is that which is supported by the Traditions contained in such works as the *Qiṣaṣu'l Anbiyá*[2] and the *'Aráisu't Tíján*[3]. In these books we are told that, when the Jews were besieging the house in which Jesus and His Apostles were, Gabriel took Jesus away through the roof or a window and carried Him off *alive* to the fourth heaven. Shuyûgh, "King of the Jews," or a friend of his called Faltianus, entering the house to slay Jesus, was mistaken for Him and put to death. But nevertheless Jesus must die, and will return to earth to do so, and that is what is implied by Sûrahs III., 48; XIX., 34; and also by Sûrah IV., 157, *if* this latter passage ("And there shall not be one of the People of the Book who shall not believe in Him before *His death*") refers to Christ's death, as many think. For "when Dajjâl[4] the Accursed comes forth[5] and misleads and makes infidels of people, and the Imâm Mahdî with a number of Muslims shall be in Jerusalem, then Jesus shall come forth and wage war with Dajjâl, and shall slay him,

[1] Weil, *Biblische Legenden der Muselmänner*, pp. 296 sqq.

[2] *Op. cit.*, pp. 274, 275.

[3] *Op. cit.*, pp. 549, 550.

[4] This is the title of Antichrist.

[5] *Qiṣaṣu'l Anbiyâ*, p. 275; cf. *'Arâisu't Tíján*, p. 554.

and shall invite His own followers to accept the Muḥammadan religion. Jesus will be of the Muḥammadan faith, and He will give quarter to every one who believes in Islâm, but He will slay every one who does not believe in Islâm. From the East even unto the West shall He subdue the whole world and make its people Musalmâns, and He shall set forth the validity of the Muḥammadan religion to such a degree that in the whole world there shall not remain a single Infidel, and the world shall be fully civilized and richly blessed. And He shall perfect justice, so that the wolf and the elk shall drink water together, and He shall be wroth with the evildoers. Then, having in this way for forty years improved the world, He too shall taste the bitterness of death and shall leave the world. Then the Musalmâns shall bury Him near the chamber of Muḥammad the Chosen One."

What is said about the return of Christ and the establishment of His kingdom over the whole earth is evidently in accordance with and borrowed from Holy Scripture, especially from such passages as Acts i. 11; Rev. 1. 7; Isa. xi. 1–10. But alas! "the trail of the Serpent is over it all," for it is asserted that *Christ shall spread Islâm with the sword*! The reference to the overthrow of Antichrist is evidently based upon 2 Thess. ii. 8–10, and similar passages. But we must inquire from what source Muḥammad has derived the idea that, after His second Advent, *Christ is to die*, if this is really the meaning of the verses from the Qur'ân which we have quoted, and if any reliance is to be placed upon the Traditions which Baihaqî and others record as handed down from Muḥammad's lips to that effect: for every Christian knows that such a fancy is absolutely contrary to Scripture (e.g. Rev. i. 17, 18).

Here again certain Apocryphal works come to our aid. In an Arabic book (probably of Coptic origin) called "The Decease of our holy Father the old man Joseph the Carpenter," we are told regarding Enoch and Elijah, who ascended into heaven without dying, that "These men must come to the world at the end of time, in the day of trouble and fear and difficulty and oppression, and must die" (cap. xxxi.)[1]. In a somewhat similar Coptic work entitled "The History of the Falling Asleep of Mary" we read almost the same words, "But as for these others" (Enoch and Elijah) "it is necessary for them also finally to taste of death[2]." Muḥammad must have heard some such expression, for he says twice over in the Qur'ân (Sûrah III., Âl 'Imrâm, 182, and Sûrah XXIX., Al 'Ankabût, 57), "Every soul doth taste of death." Holding, as he apparently did, that Jesus ascended to heaven alive (Sûrah III., 48), it naturally followed, to his mind, that Christ also,

[1] ينبغي لأولئك يأتوا الى العالم في آخر الزمان في يوم القلق والخوف والشدّة والضيق ويموتوا

[2] *Coptic Apocryphal Gospels*, pp. 108, 109.

like Enoch and Elijah, would necessarily die after his second Advent. Hence Christ's vacant tomb now lies ready for Him at Medina, between the graves of Muḥammad and Abû Bakr!

Muḥammadan Tradition also tells us that Christ shall take a wife after His return[1]. This is due to a misunderstanding of such passages as Rev. xix. 7–9, where we read: "Let us rejoice and be exceeding glad, and let us give the glory unto Him: for the marriage of the Lamb is come, and His wife hath made herself ready. And it was given unto her that she should array herself in fine linen, bright and pure: for the fine linen is the righteous acts of the saints. And he saith unto me, Blessed are they which are bidden to the marriage supper of the Lamb." Of course the meaning of this allegorical passage is fully explained elsewhere (e.g. Rev. xxi. 2; Eph. v. 22–32) as referring to the perfect love and complete union in spiritual matters which will then exist between the Saviour and His purified and redeemed Church.

The statement that Christ is to live *forty years*[2] on the earth after His return must have originated in a misunderstanding of Acts i. 3, where we learn that He remained for *forty days* with His disciples after His Resurrection and before His Ascension.

[1] *'Arâisu'l Majâlis*, p. 554.

[2] *Qiṣaṣu'l Anbiyâ*, p. 275.

7. *Christ's supposed prediction of the coming of Muḥammad.*

There are a considerable number of passages in the Bible which Muḥammadan controversialists endeavour to prove to be prophecies of Muḥammad. But we have here to deal with only one small series of verses, since only in one place in the Qur'ân do we find a clear assertion that Christ told His disciples to look for Muḥammad's appearance; and it is to certain verses in St. John's Gospel that he evidently refers. In Sûrah LXI., Aṣ Ṣaff, 6, Muḥammad writes thus:—

"And when Jesus, Son of Mary, said, 'O Children of Israel, verily I am the Apostle of God unto you, confirming what was before Me of the Law, and proclaiming good tidings of an Apostle who shall come after Me: his name is Aḥmad.'"

The reference here is to the coming of the Paraclete or "Comforter" spoken of in John xiv. 16, 26; xv. 26; xvi. 7. We have already[1] pointed out that Muḥammad was misled by some ignorant but zealous proselyte or other disciple, who confounded the word Παράκλητος used in these verses with another Greek word περικλυτός, which might, without a *very* great stretch of the imagination, be interpreted by the Arabic word Aḥmad, "the greatly praised," only, unfortunately for Muḥammad, περικλυτός *is not the word used*, and by no possible effort

[1] p. 142, note 1.

can the term employed by our Lord be translated Aḥmad. "A little knowledge," even of Greek, may be "a dangerous thing;" and certainly the proverb was never better illustrated than in the Qur'ân. Of course everyone who reads the passages in St. John's Gospel at all carefully will perceive that they contain no prophecy of any coming Prophet, and cannot possibly be made to suit any mere human being. Moreover, every Christian knows how the promise was fulfilled (Acts ii. 1–11). It is quite a mistake, on the other hand, to fancy that Muḥammad claimed to be the Holy Spirit, whom the Muslims confound with Gabriel.

Before leaving this subject it may be as well to remind the reader that Muḥammad was not the first to appeal to these verses as a prophecy of himself. It is well known that Mânî[1] or Manes, renowned in Persian fable as a wonderful painter, made the same claim to be the "person" referred to by Christ. Only Mânî distinctly claimed to be the "Paraclete," probably (like Muḥammad) in order to win over ill-informed Christians to his side. This is remarkable, for he rejected the historical Jesus and invented another for himself, who neither suffered nor died (*Jesus impassibilis*). A third point in which he resembled Muḥammad was his claim to be the last and greatest of the pro-

[1] Manichaism had taken refuge in Arabia long before Muḥammad's time (Beausobre, *Histoire du Manichéisme*, Pt. I, ch. iv.).

phets, "the Ambassador of Light," which he identified with the Deity. He was less fortunate than Muḥammad, however, since he was impaled by the command of Bahrâm I, of Persia, about 276 A.D.[1]. Finally, he produced a book, called *Artang*[2] by Oriental writers, which he said had been sent down to him from heaven and contained the final revelation to men. His denial of Christ's sufferings originated in his acceptance of the Gnostic idea of the essential evil of all matter, and this made him deny that the true Jesus had a human body. In this respect he followed Basilides more logically than did Muḥammad, as we have already seen.

8. *Creation of Adam, and his being worshipped by the Angels.*

In Sûrah III., Âl 'Imrân, 52, we read:—

"Verily the likeness of Jesus, according to God, is as the likeness of Adam;" and of the latter it is then added: "He created him out of earth; then He said to him, 'Be'; therefore he comes into being[3]."

With regard to the creation of Adam out of the

[1] Most of our information about Mânî himself comes from *Al Fihrist*, though it is difficult to say on what authorities the author of that work relied. Mânî was born probably in A.D. 216. Patristic writers give much information about his teaching.

[2] Perhaps meaning "The Noble Tome," from *Arta* (Av. *ereta*) + *añga*, limb, portion.

[3] See note 2 to p. 55 above.

soil, Tradition tells us that when God Most High wished to create him, He sent one after another of the Archangels to take and bring Him a handful of earth. The Earth, knowing that many of Adam's descendants would be condemned to hell fire, adjured each of these messengers not to take away any portion of her substance. Hence they all except the last, 'Azrâîl, returned empty-handed. 'Azrâîl, however, took a handful of earth in spite of this adjuration, some say from the spot upon which the Ka'bah was afterwards built, others from the whole surface of the earth. He brought it to God[1], saying, "O God, Thou knowest: lo! I have brought it." Abû'l Fidâ, on the authority of Kâmil ibn Athîr, says, "The Prophet of God said, 'Verily God Most High created Adam from a handful which He took from the whole of the Earth, . . . and truly he was called Adam because he was created from the surface (*adîm*) of the Earth.' "

This Tradition is interesting because it affords another instance of how much Islâm is indebted to heretical ideas. The whole fable is borrowed from Marcion, as we learn from a quotation from one of the latter's writings which is given in Ezniq the Armenian's work entitled *The Refutation of Heresies*. In speaking of this heresiarch of the second century, Ezniq quotes[2] the following passage as containing some of his peculiar views, "And

[1] *Qiṣaṣu'l Anbiyá*, p. 11.

[2] Book IV.

when the God of the Law saw that this world was beautiful, He resolved to make Man out of it. And having descended unto the Earth, unto Matter (ὕλη), He saith, 'Give Me of thy clay and I shall give spirit from Myself.' . . . When Matter had given Him of her earth, He created him (Adam), and breathed spirit into him. . . . And on this account he was named Adam, because he was made out of clay."

To understand this quotation we must remember that Marcion held the old Persian dualism to a great extent, believing that there are two First Causes, one perfectly good and the other perfectly evil. The Demiurgos or Creator of this lower world, who is here spoken of as the God of the Law because he gave the Law of Moses to the Jews, is just, but neither perfectly good nor perfectly evil, yet he is perpetually at war with the Evil Principle. He is therefore rather an archangel than a God, and in the Muḥammadan legend appears as such. According to Marcion's view, the Demiurgos originally dwelt in the second heaven and was not at first aware of the existence of the Supreme Principle of Good, whom Marcion called the Unknown God. When he learnt His existence, the Demiurgos became hostile to Him, and began to try to prevent men from knowing God, lest they should transfer their worship to Him. Therefore the Supreme God sent Jesus Christ into the world to destroy the power of the God of the

Law and that of the Evil Principle, and to lead men to a knowledge of the True God. Jesus was attacked by both these beings, but they could not hurt Him, as he had only the appearance of a body, so that He might be visible to men, not a real body. Here again we find the Docetic principle which, though so contrary to Muḥammad's general teaching, yet underlies the denial of the crucifixion of Christ.

Much of what Marcion said about the Demiurgos agrees with the Muḥammadan legend about 'Azâzîl, who became an inhabitant of the second heaven (and, according to some Traditions, of all the heavens) before he was cast out and received the names of Iblîs (Διάβολος) and Shaiṭân (Satan). But both Marcion's and Muḥammad's statements on this point are so evidently borrowed from Zoroastrian legends that we must reserve them for treatment in our next chapter[1].

It is worthy of note that to the Demiurgos the titles of "Lord of the Worlds," "Creator of the Creatures," and "Prince of this World," were given by Marcion and his followers. The first two of these titles properly belong to God, and are used for Him by both Jews and Muslims. The third is borrowed from John xiv. 30, where it is given to Satan. Through an unfortunate mistake, Muḥammadans understand this verse as a prophecy re-

[1] pp. 242, sqq.

garding Muḥammad, and apply this title to their Prophet in consequence!

In connexion with the creation of Adam, the Qur'ân repeatedly asserts that God commanded the angels to worship him. Among other verses to this effect we may adduce the following:—

Sûrah II., Al Baqarah, 32, "And when We said to the angels, 'Worship Adam,' then they worshipped him, except Iblîs."

Sûrahs XVII., Al Asra', 63; XVIII., Al Kahf, 48; and XX., Ṭa Ha, 115, contain the same statement in almost the same words.

This idea can hardly be derived from the Talmud, in which, though we are told that the angels showed Adam undue respect, yet it is distinctly stated that they did wrong. It is doubtless borrowed from a misapprehension of Heb. i. 6: "And again, when He bringeth in the first-begotten into the world, He saith, 'And let all the angels of God worship Him.'" Muḥammad seems to have been greatly struck with this verse, and, since he (as usual) misunderstood it by fancying that "the first-begotten[1]" meant not Christ but Adam, he repeatedly introduced its equivalent into the Qur'ân. This may have been done as an argument against worship being offered to Christ, for in a verse already quoted (Sûrah III., 52) he tells us

[1] Probably Muḥammad confounded the 'first-*begotten*" of this passage with the term "first-*created*" repeatedly applied to Adam in the "Testament of Abraham": vide below, p. 208.

that in God's sight Jesus was just as Adam, doubtless in having no human father (as 'Abbâsî and Jalâlain explain it), but that He was not to be accounted Divine on that account.

9. *All must go down into Hell.*

This strange idea is thus expressed in Sûrah XIX., Maryam, 69–73:—

"Therefore, by thy Lord! We shall surely assemble them and the devils, then We shall surely make them present, kneeling, around Hell. Then shall We take out from each sect whoso of them is most violent in rebellion against the Merciful One. Then indeed We are best aware concerning those who shall be first in it in burning: and there is none of you but goeth down into it. It has become concerning thy Lord a fixed decision."

This passage has caused much unhappiness to pious Muslims, even though they *hope* that the fire of hell will not injure them. Commentators have striven manfully to explain away the obvious meaning of the words by saying (though they are by no means agreed in this opinion) that what is meant is merely that all men, even true Muslims, must come near to hell fire, and that they do this when they pass over the Bridge[1] Aṣ Ṣirâṭ on the Judgment Day. If this explanation be accepted, the passage should be dealt with in Chapter v,

[1] pp. 251, sqq.

when we are considering Zoroastrian influence on the origin of Islâm. But it is more probable from the language of the verses we have quoted that here Muḥammad expresses his belief in Purgatory. If so, he must have learnt this from the Christians of his day. Attempts have been made to deduce this doctrine from Mark ix. 49 and 1 Cor. iii. 13. It is *possible*, of course, that Muḥammad had heard these verses read, and that he misunderstood them in this sense; but it is far more likely that he borrowed the error ready made. The "Testament of Abraham" tells us that each man's work is tried by fire, and that, if the fire burns up any man's work, he is carried off to the place of torture by the angel who presides over fire. As, however, the meaning of this isolated passage in the Qur'ân is somewhat uncertain, we need not inquire further into the origin of the doctrine of Purgatory.

10. *The "Balance."*

Mention is made of the Balance (in which good deeds and bad are to be weighed at the Last Day) in several places in the Qur'ân, the chief of which are:—

Sûrah VII., Al A'râf, 7, 8: "And the weighing on that day shall be truth: therefore he whose scales are heavy—those are accordingly the prosperous; and he whose scales are light—those are accordingly those who shall have lost their own souls."

Sûrah XXI., Al Anbiyâ, 48: "And We shall set the just scales for the Day of the Resurrection, therefore a soul shall not be wronged in anything; and if it were the weight of a grain of mustard We should bring it; and it sufficeth with Us as accountants."

Sûrah XLII., Ash Shûra', 16: "It is God who hath sent down the Book with truth, and the Balance."

Sûrah CI., Al Qâri'ah, 5, 6: "Therefore as for him whose scales are heavy, he shall consequently be in a happy life; and as for him whose scales are light, his mother (*i.e.* abode) shall be lowest hell."

Commentators, on the authority of Tradition, explain these verses by informing us that on the Resurrection Day God will erect between Heaven and Earth a Balance having a tongue and two scales or pans. This will be reserved exclusively for the task of weighing men's good deeds and their bad ones, or the records in which these are set down. True believers will see that the scale into which their good deeds are cast will outweigh the other, which contains their evil deeds: while the scale containing the good deeds of unbelievers will be light, being outweighed by their evil ones. Not the very slightest good act of the believer will be left out of the account, nor will anything be added to his sins. Those whose good deeds preponderate will enter Paradise, but those whose good actions are outbalanced by their evil ones will be cast into Hell fire.

It has been pointed out that the idea of weighing men's actions occurs in the Talmud, e.g. in Rôsh Hashshânâh, cap. 17. It may there be derived from Daniel v. 27. But in this case the balance spoken of is a metaphorical one, and the "weighing" of Belshazzar does not take place on the Resurrection Day, or even after his death, but while he is still alive. We must look elsewhere for the origin of the Muḥammadan conception, and we find it once more in an apocryphal book, the "Testament of Abraham [1]." This work seems to have been originally written in Egypt. It was known to Origen, and was probably composed either in the second century of our era, or not later than the third, by a Jewish convert to Christianity. It exists in two Greek recensions and also in an Arabic version. The resemblance between certain passages in this book and certain verses of the Qur'ân and also later Muḥammadan Tradition is too great to be merely fortuitous [2]. This is especially observable in what is told us in the "Testament of Abraham" in reference to the "Balance."

It is there stated that when the Angel of Death came by God's command to take away Abraham's

[1] Published in *Texts and Studies*, vol. ii, no. 2.

[2] See examples in *The Religion of the Crescent*, Appendix C, pp. 242 sqq.

spirit, the patriarch made request that before dying he should be permitted to behold the marvels of heaven and earth. Permission being granted, he ascended to the sky under the leadership of the angel, and saw all things that were to be seen. When he reached the second heaven, he there perceived the Balance in which an angel weighs men's deeds, as the following passage explains:—

"In[1] the midst of the two gates stood a throne, ... and on it sat a marvellous man ... and before him stood a table like unto crystal, all of gold and fine linen. And on the table lay a book, its thickness was six cubits and its breadth ten cubits. And to the right and left of it (the table) there stood two[2] angels, holding paper and ink and a pen. And in front of the table was seated a light-bearing angel, holding a Balance in his hand; and to the left sat a fiery angel, altogether merciless and stern, holding in his hand a trumpet, in which he kept an all-consuming fire, the test of sinners. And the marvellous man who was seated on the throne was himself judging and proving the souls, but the two angels who were on the right and on the left were registering: the one on the right was registering the righteous acts, but the one on the

[1] "Testament of Abraham," Recension A, cap. xii, p. 91: cf. pp. 92, 93. 113. 114, capp. xiii, xiv, and Recension B, cap. vii.

[2] Cf. Sûrah L., 16, 17, 20.

left the sins. And the one in front of the table, the one who held the Balance, was weighing the souls; and the fiery angel who held the fire was testing the souls. And Abraham asked Michael, the general-in-chief, 'What are these things that we are beholding?' And the general-in-chief said, 'What thou seest, holy Abraham, is the judgment and retribution.'"

The narrative goes on to state that Abraham saw that every soul whose good and bad deeds were equal was reckoned neither among the saved nor among the lost, but took his stand in a place between the two. This latter matter completely agrees with Muḥammadan belief, which is said to rest upon Sûrah VII., Al A'râf, 44: "And between them both" (heaven and hell) "is a veil, and upon the A'râf are men," and is also based upon Tradition.

It seems impossible to doubt that Muḥammad was indebted, directly or indirectly, for his teaching about the Balance to this apocryphal work, or to the same idea prevalent orally at the time and ultimately derived from Egypt. The probability is that he learnt it from Mary, his Coptic concubine. The conception of such a Balance for weighing men's deeds, good and bad, is a very ancient one in Egypt. We find it in the "Judgment Scene" of the *Book of the Dead,* so many copies of which have been found in ancient Egyptian tombs. Regarding this work Dr. Budge says, "It[1] is quite certain that the *Book of the Dead*, in a connected form, is as old as Egyptian civilization, and that its sources belong to prehistoric times to which it is impossible to assign a date. We first touch solid ground in the history of the *Book of the Dead* in the period of the early dynasties, and, if we accept one tradition which was current in Egypt as early as B.C. 2,500, we are right in believing that certain parts of it are, in their present form, as old as the time of the First Dynasty." Regarding its authorship he says, "From[2] time immemorial the god Thoth, who was both the Divine Intelligence which at creation uttered the words that were carried into effect by Ptaḥ and Khnemu, and the Scribe of the Gods, was associated with the production of the *Book of the Dead*." The object of burying a copy of this Book along with the mummy was that the dead man might receive instruction from it and learn how to avoid the various dangers he would encounter in the next world. We learn from it a great deal of the religious ideas of the Egyptians. The vignette which represents the Judgment of the soul, which probably (as in the "Testament of Abraham") took place soon after death, varies in different copies, though they all preserve the same general outline. A form which is often found[3] shows us two gods, Horus and Anubis, engaged in

[1] *The Book of the Dead*, vol. iii, p. xlvii. [2] *Op. cit.*, p. lxxv.
[3] *Vide* Note, p. 8 above.

weighing a man's heart in one scale of the Balance against the image of Maāt, the goddess of Truth and Right, which is placed in the other scale. Another god, Thoth—in Egyptian *Tehûti*—is writing down the dead man's account on a scroll. Over the Balance is written: "The Osiris lives justified. In its place the Balance is level in the midst of the Divine Judgment-Hall. He says, 'As for his heart, let his heart enter into its place in Osiris *so and so* the Justified.' May Thoth, the great god in the city of Ḥeseret, lord of the city Hermopolis, lord of the words of Thoth, say this." The bestowal of the name of *Osiris* on the dead man as well as his own name (for the insertion of which a place is left vacant) signifies that, being justified in the judgment, he has become identified with the god Osiris, the supreme deity of the ancient Egyptians, and is therefore safe from the assaults of the evil powers.

In front of the figure of the divine scribe Thoth stands a terrible animal, something like a bitch. This was supposed to devour the wicked. Over its head is written, "Conqueror of enemies by swallowing them, lady of Hades, hound of Hades." Near this animal there stands an altar full of offerings, placed in front of the entrance to the inner shrine. Within the shrine, seated on a throne, is Osiris himself, the "Good Being," holding in one hand a sceptre and in the other a scourge. He sits as judge, prepared to deal with the dead man's spirit according to what Thoth may write in the roll regarding the result of weighing his heart in the Balance. In front of Osiris is an inscription containing some of his titles. It may be read thus: "Osiris, the Good Being, God, Lord of Life, the great God, Lord of futurity, Chief of Paradise and Hell, in Hades, the great God, Lord of the city of Ȧbṭ, king of past eternity, God." Beneath his throne the words "Life and Health" are written several times.

It is evident from a comparison of this picture with what we have read in the "Testament of Abraham" and in the Qur'ân that the "Balance" mentioned in the Qur'ân and the Traditions of Muḥammad is ultimately derived from the ancient Egyptian mythology, through the medium of Coptic Christian ideas[1] which are mentioned in the "Testament of Abraham," having been handed down orally during generation after generation in Egypt, the land of their birth.

[1] In Zoroastrian mythology also the Balance appears in a manner very similar to its use in Egyptian. Rashnu, one of the three judges of the dead (cf. the Greek story of the same duty assigned to Minos, Rhadamanthus and Aeacus, in Plato's *Gorgias*, cap. lxxix) holds a Balance, and in it men's good deeds and bad are weighed after their death. The other judges are Mithra and Sraosha, the Mihr and Sarôsh of later Persian legends. In the Middle Ages in Europe Michael was supposed to hold the Balance.

11. *Adam's joy and grief in Heaven.*

In Sûrah XVII., Al Asrâ', 1, we read a brief account of Muḥammad's mythical journey to heaven, which occupies a very extensive place in Muḥammadan Tradition. The words of this verse may be rendered thus:—

"Praise be to Him who caused His servant to journey by night from the Sacred Mosque[1] to the Farther Mosque[2], whose enclosure We have blessed, that We might show him of Our signs."

Regarding this *Mi'râj* of Muḥammad, as it is called, we shall have to treat at some length in the next chapter[3]. Here we refer to it in order to introduce a Tradition concerning one part of Muḥammad's experience on that famous journey. In the *Mishkâtu'l Maṣâbîḥ* we are told of a scene which he saw on entering the lowest of the seven Heavens:—

"Then[4] when He opened to us the lowest heaven, lo! a man seated: at his right hand were black figures and at his left hand were black figures. When he glanced towards his right he laughed, and when he glanced towards his left he wept. . . I said to Gabriel, 'Who is this.' He said, 'This is Adam, and these black figures on his right hand and on his left hand are the souls of his

[1] The Ka'bah at Mecca.

[2] The Temple at Jerusalem!

[3] Pp. 218 sqq.

[4] *Op. cit.*, p. 521.

children; and those of them that are on the right are to be the people of Paradise, and the black figures which are on his left are to be the people of the Fire. Therefore when he looked towards his right he laughed, and when he looked towards his left side he wept.'"

This Tradition also may be traced back to the apocryphal "Testament of Abraham," as the following extract proves:—

"Michael[1] turned the chariot and carried Abraham towards the East, at the first gate of Heaven. And Abraham saw two ways; the one way strait and narrow and the other broad and wide; and there he saw two gates, one gate broad, corresponding to the broad way, and one gate strait, corresponding to the strait way. And outside of the two gates there I saw a man seated upon a throne covered with gold: and the appearance of that person was terrible, like unto the Lord. And I saw many souls being driven by angels and being led through the broad gate; and I saw other souls, a few, and they were being borne by angels through the strait gate. And when the marvellous man who was seated on the golden throne saw few entering through the strait gate but many entering through the broad gate, immediately that marvellous man seized the hair of his head and the sides of his beard and hurled himself from the throne to the ground, weeping

[1] "Testament of Abraham," Recension A, cap. xi.

and wailing. And when he saw many souls entering through the strait gate, then he would rise up from the ground and seat himself upon his throne in great gladness, rejoicing and exulting. Abraham asked the general-in-chief" (the archangel Michael), "'My lord, the general-in-chief, who is this altogether marvellous man who is adorned with such splendour, and who at one time weeps and wails, but at another rejoices and exults?' The bodiless one said, 'This is Adam, the first created person, who is in such glory, and he beholds the world, since all were (born) from him: and when he sees many souls entering through the strait gate, then he rises and sits down upon his throne, rejoicing and exulting in gladness, because this strait gate is that of the just, which leadeth unto life, and those who enter through it go into Paradise: and on this account does Adam the first-created rejoice, because he perceives souls being saved. And when he sees many souls entering through the broad gate, then he rends the hair of his head and hurls himself to the ground, weeping and wailing bitterly. For the broad gate is that of sinners, which leads unto destruction and unto eternal punishment.'"

12. *Borrowings from the New Testament.*

Finally it may be asked, Has Muḥammad borrowed nothing from the New Testament itself, since he has derived such a considerable amount of his teaching from apocryphal Christian sources?

In answer to this we are obliged to admit that he borrowed very little indeed from the New Testament. From it he may be said *indirectly* to have learnt that Jesus was born without a human father, that He had a Divine commission, wrought miracles, had a number of Apostles, and ascended to heaven. Muḥammad denied the Deity, the atoning death (and consequently the Resurrection) of Christ, and taught a great deal that was contrary to the leading doctrines of the Gospel, being desirous of himself supplanting Christ and prevailing on men to admit his own claim to be the last and greatest of the Messengers of God. We have seen that in the Qur'ân and the Traditions we find distorted references to certain passages of the New Testament, as for instance in what is said about the descent of the Table, and the supposed prophecy of Muḥammad's coming. But there is only one passage in the Qur'ân which may be said to contain a direct quotation from the Gospels. This is found in Sûrah VII., Al A'râf, 38, where we read:—

"Verily they who have accused Our signs of falsehood . . ., unto them the gates of heaven shall not be opened, nor shall they enter Paradise *until the camel entereth in at the eye of the needle.*" This is almost a literal quotation from Luke xviii. 25: "It is easier for a camel to enter in through a needle's eye, than for a rich man to enter into the kingdom of God." Very similar words occur also in Matt. xix. 24, and Mark x. 25.

In the Traditions, moreover, there is one striking instance of a quotation from the Epistles, and it is a favourite with many thoughtful Muslims, who have not the slightest idea that it comes from the Bible. Abû Hurairah is reported[1] to have attributed to Muḥammad the statement that God Most High had said: I have *prepared* for My righteous servants *what eye hath not seen nor ear heard, nor hath it occurred to the heart of a human being.*" It will be readily recognized that these words are a quotation from 1 Cor. ii. 9. Whether Abû Hurairah, surnamed the Liar, has spoken the truth in asserting that he heard this passage quoted by Muḥammad may well be doubted. Yet the passage in Sûrah LXXV., 22, 23, "Faces in that day shall be brightened, gazing at their Lord," which refers to the Beatific Vision[2], and is a reminiscence of 1 John iii. 2, and 1 Cor. xiii. 12, lends some support to his statement.

From a careful examination of the whole subject dealt with in this chapter we therefore conclude that the influence of true and genuine Christian teaching upon the Qur'ân and upon Islâm in general has been very slight indeed, while on the

[1] *Mishkâtu'l Maṣâbîḥ*, p. 487.

[2] On the Muḥammadan idea of this, vide *The Religion of the Crescent*, pp. 116, 118.

other hand apocryphal traditions and in certain respects heretical doctrines have a claim to be considered as forming one of the original sources of the Muḥammadan faith[1].

[1] In his *Muhammadanische Studien* (vol. II, pp. 382 sqq.) Professor Goldziher has an interesting account of the way in which in later times "Traditions" were borrowed from Christian sources. But this lies beyond our present inquiry.

CHAPTER V.

ZOROASTRIAN ELEMENTS IN THE QUR'ÂN AND TRADITIONS OF ISLÂM.

THE political influence which the Persians exercised over certain parts of the Arabian Peninsula and the neighbouring countries in and before Muḥammad's time was very considerable, as we learn from Arabian and Greek writers alike. Abû'l Fidâ, for example, informs us that, early in the seventh century of the Christian era, Khusrau (or, as the Arabs called him, Kisra') Anûshîravân, the great Persian conqueror, invaded the kingdom of Ḥîrah on the banks of the Euphrates, dethroned the king Ḥârith, and placed upon the throne in his stead a creature of his own, named Mundhir Mâi's Samâ. Not long afterwards Anûshîravân sent an army into Yaman, under a general called Vahraz, to expel the Abyssinians who had taken possession of the country, and to restore the Yamanite prince Abû's Saif to the throne of his ancestors [1]. But the Persian force remained in the country, and its general ultimately himself ascended the throne and handed it down to his descendants [2]. Abû'l Fidâ tells us [3] that

[1] *Abû'l Fidâ*, cap. ii.

[2] *Sîratu'r Rasûl*, pp. 24, 25.

[3] *Ut supra:* كانت المناذرة آل نصر بن ربيعة عمالاً للاكاسرة على عرب العراق

the princes of the family of Mundhir who succeeded him in Ḥîrah, and ruled also over the Arabian 'Irâq, were merely governors under the kings of Persia. He says with reference to Yaman that four Abyssinian rulers and eight Persian princes held sway there before it acknowledged Muḥammad's[1] sovereignty. But even earlier than Muḥammad's time there was much intercourse between the North-West and West of Arabia and the Persian dominions. We are informed that Naufal and Muṭṭalab (who were the brothers of Muḥammad's great-grandfather), when they were the leading chiefs of the Quraish, made a treaty with the Persians, by which the merchants of Mecca were permitted to trade with 'Irâq and Fârs (the ancient Persis). In the year 606, or about that time, a party of merchants headed by Abû Sufyân reached the Persian capital and were received into the king's presence[2].

When Muḥammad laid claim to the prophetic office in 612 A.D., the Persians had overrun and held possession for a time of Syria, Palestine, and Asia Minor. At the time of the Hijrah in A.D. 622, the Emperor Heraclius had begun to retrieve the fortunes of the Byzantine Empire, and not long after the Persians were obliged to sue for peace.

[1] ثم ملك اليمن بعدهم من الحبشة اربعة ومن الفرس ثمانية ثم صارت اليمن للاسلام

[2] Sir W. Muir, *Life of Mahomet*, pp. xcvii and 31, 32.

In consequence of this, Bâdzan, the Persian governor of Yaman, deprived of the hope of support from home, was obliged to submit to Muḥammad and agree to pay tribute (A. D. 628). Within a few years of the Prophet's death the armies of Islâm had overrun Persia and converted the great mass of its people by the sword.

Whenever two nations, the one highly advanced in civilization and the other in a state of comparative ignorance, are brought into close intercourse with one another, the former always exercises a very considerable influence over the other. All history teaches us this lesson. Now in Muḥammad's time the Arabs were in a very unenlightened condition; in fact their own writers speak of pre-Islâmic ages as "The Times of Ignorance." The Persians, on the other hand, as we learn from the Avestâ, from the cuneiform inscriptions of Darius and Xerxes, from the still existing ruins of Persepolis, and from the evidence of Greek writers, had from at least very early times been highly civilized. It was but natural therefore that intercourse with them should leave its impress upon the Arabs. From Arabian historians and from the statements of the Qur'ân and its commentators it is evident that the romantic legends and the poetry of the Persians had in Muḥammad's time obtained a very considerable degree of popularity among the Arabs. So widely were some of these tales known among the

Quraish that Muḥammad was accused by his enemies of having borrowed or imitated them in the Qur'ân. Ibn Hishâm, for instance, says that one day when Muḥammad "had gathered an assembly, then he summoned them to God Most High and read the Qur'ân there, and warned them what would befall the nations that remained destitute of faith. Then Naḍr bin Al Ḥârith, who had followed him into his assembly, rose up and told them about Rustam the strong and about Isfandiyâr and the kings of Persia. Then he said, 'By God! Muḥammad is not a better story-teller than I am, and his discourse is nothing but the Tales of the Ancients. He has composed them just as I have composed them.' On his account therefore did God send down the verse: 'And[1] they have said, Tales of the Ancients hath he written down, and they are recited to him morning and evening. Say thou, He who knoweth what is secret in the heavens and the earth hath sent it down: verily He is forgiving, merciful.' And on his account this also came down: 'When[2] our verses are recited to him, he hath said, Tales of the Ancients!' And this also descended for his benefit: 'Woe[3] unto every sinful liar that heareth God's verses read to him; then he persisteth in being proud, as if he did not hear them! There-

[1] Sûrah XXV., Al Furqân, 6, 7.
[2] Sûrah LXVIII., 15.
[3] Sûrah XLV., 6, 7.

fore give him good news of a sore punishment[1].""

Muḥammad's answer to the charge thus brought against him cannot have been altogether satisfactory to his audience, nor can we deem it sufficient to deter us from inquiring whether an examination of certain passages of the Qur'ân does not bear out the assertion thus made by his early opponents.

The stories of "Rustam and Isfandiyâr and the Kings of Persia" which were referred to by Naḍr are doubtless among those which, some generations later, Firdausî, the most celebrated of the epic poets of Persia, learnt from the collection which he tells us a Persian villager had made, and which Firdausî has left us in poetic form in the

[1] والنضر بن الحارث بن كلدة بن علقمة بن عبد مناف بن عبد الدار بن قصي كان اذا جلس رسول الله صلى الله عليهِ وسلم مجلساً فدعا فيه الى الله تعالى وتلا فيه القرآن وحذر قريشاً ما اصاب الامم الخالية خلفهُ في مجلسه اذا قام فحدّثهم عن رستم الشديد وعن اسفنديار وملوك فارس ثم يقول والله ما محمد باحسن حديثاً مني وما حديثه الّا اساطير الاولين اكتتبها كما اكتتبتُها فانزل الله فيه "وقالوا اساطيرُ الاولين اكتتبها فهي تُملى عليهِ بكرةً واصيلاً قلْ أنزلهُ ٱلذي يعلمُ السرّ في السمواتِ والارضِ انهُ كان غفوراً رحيماً" ونزل فيهِ "اذا تتلى عليهِ آياتنا قال أساطير الاولين" ونزل فيهِ "ويلٌ لكلِّ افاكٍ أثيم يسمعُ آياتِ اللهِ تتلى عليهِ ثم يُصِرّ مستكبراً كأن لم يسمعها فبشّرْهُ بعذاب أليم" (*Sîratu'r Rasûl.*)

Shâhnâmeh. Doubtless all these tales are very ancient in some form, but we need not depend upon the *Shâhnâmeh* for those which we shall have to quote or refer to; and this is well, because the authority of a work, which, in its present poetical form, is later than Muḥammad's time, might not be deemed sufficient. Fortunately in the Avestâ and other books of the Pârsîs or Zoroastrians we have information which cannot be called in question on the ground of antiquity, and it is to these we shall appeal.

It may be safely concluded that, since the tales of the kings of Persia were of interest to the Arabs and they had heard of Rustam and Isfandiyâr, they are unlikely to have been quite ignorant of the story of Jamshîd. Nor is it probable that the Persian fables regarding the ascension to heaven of Artâ Vîrâf and of Zoroaster before him, their descriptions of Paradise and the Bridge of Chinvaṭ and the tree Ḥvâpah, the legend of Ahriman's coming up out of primaeval darkness, and many other such marvellous tales, had remained entirely unknown to the Arabs. If they were known, it was natural that Muḥammad should have made some use of them, as he did of Christian and Jewish legends. We must therefore inquire whether such fancies have left any trace upon the Qur'ân and the Traditions current among the Muslims. We shall see that not only is this the case, but that in some instances these

Persian tales are so indubitably of Âryan and not of Semitic origin that they are found in slightly modified forms in India also. In fact some of them were, so to speak, part of the religious and intellectual heritage of both nations; and when the Persians and the Hindûs separated from one another, and, leaving their ancient common home —the Airyanem Vaêjô [1]—near Herât, migrated to Persia and India respectively, were carried away in the minds of both peoples. Others of these ideas may very possibly have originated in Persia somewhat later, and have spread to India in process of time. We shall see that they had certainly reached Muḥammad's ears, and they have not been without influence upon the Qur'ân and the Traditions, which claim to have been handed down by his devoted followers, relating what they assert that they heard from his lips.

1. *The Night Journey.*

The first matter with which we shall here deal is the celebrated account of Muḥammad's *Night Journey.* This is thus referred to in a verse which we have already [2] quoted (Sûrah XVII., Al Asra'— also called Sûrah Banî Isrâîl'—1):—

"Praise be to Him who caused His servant to journey by night from the Sacred Mosque to the Farther Mosque, whose enclosure We have blessed, that We might show him of Our signs."

[1] *Vendidâd,* I., 1, 2, &c. [2] pp. 206, 207.

It is well known that commentators on the Qur'ân are by no means agreed with regard to this verse, some thinking that Muḥammad merely dreamt that he made the journey mentioned in it, others taking it in a literal sense and adding many details from Tradition, and others again explaining it in a mystical or figurative sense. Ibn Isḥâq, for example, informs us, giving his traditional authority, that Muḥammad's favourite wife 'Âyishah used to say, "The body of the Apostle of God did not disappear, but God took his spirit on the journey by night." Another Tradition reports that Muḥammad himself said, "My[1] eye was sleeping and my heart was awake." The celebrated mystical commentator Muḥiyyu'd Dîn accepted the whole account only in a metaphorical sense[2]. As, however, we are not con-

[1] *Siratu'r Rasûl*, p. 139.

[2] For the benefit of the curious in such matters we subjoin his account, given in his comment on the verse above quoted:—

"سبحان الذي اسرى اي انزهه عن اللواحق المادية والنقائص التشبيهية بلسان حال التجرد والكمال في مقام العبودية الذي لا تصرف فيه اصلاً ليلاً اي في ظلمة الغواشى البدنية والتعلقات الطبيعية لان العروج والترقي لا يكون الا بواسطة البدن من المسجد الحرام اي من مقام القلب المحرّم عن ان يطوف به مشرك القوى البدنية ويرتكب فيه فواحشها وخطاياها ويحجه غويّ القوى الحيوانية من البهيمية والسبعية المنكشفة سواتاً افراطها وتفريطها لعروها عن لباس الفضيلة

cerned seriously to discuss the question of the actual occurrence of this "Night Journey," we need not deal further with this view. It is certain that the great mass of Muḥammadan commentators and Traditionalists believe that Muḥammad actually went from Mecca to Jerusalem and also visited the heavens, and they give long accounts, of deep and abiding interest to Muslims, regarding what he did and what he saw. It is with this Tradition that we have to deal, and we shall see that it is easy to trace the origin of its main features to earlier legends, and especially to Zoroastrian sources. This is true, whether we believe with the vast mass of Muḥammadans that Muḥammad himself gave such an account of his *Miʿrâj* as the ones we now proceed to translate, or infer that the whole legend is the production of somewhat later times[1]. We quote Ibn Isḥâq's

---

الى المسجد الأقصى الذي هو مقام الروح الا بعد من العالم الجسماني بشهود تجليات الذات وسبحات الوجه وتذكر ما ذكرنا ان تصحيح كل مقام لا يكون الا بعد الترقي الى ما فوقه لتفهم من قوله لنريه من اياتنا مشاهدة الصفات فان مطالعة تجليات الصفات وان كانت في مقام القلب لكن الذات الموصوفة بتلك الصفات لاتشاهد على الكمال بصفة الجلال الا عند الترقي الى مقام الروح اي لنريه آيات صفاتنا من جهة انها منسوبة الينا ونحن المشاهدون بها البارزون بصورها"

[1] Against this latter hypothesis, however, must be considered

account first, because it is the earliest that has reached us. It is given by Ibn Hishâm, his editor and continuator, in the following manner. Muḥammad, we are informed, asserted that Gabriel came and awoke him twice to go on the "Night Journey," but he fell asleep again. Then he continues:—

"Accordingly he (Gabriel) came to me the third time: then he touched me with his foot, and I sat up. He seized me by my arm, and I stood up with him. He then went forth to the door of the Mosque: and lo! a white animal, (in appearance) between a mule and an ass; on its flanks were two wings, with which it rules both its hind feet: its fore-foot it sets down at the limit of its glance. He mounted me upon it, then he went forth with me, (in such a way that) he does not precede me and I do not precede him. . . . When I approached it (the animal) to mount it, it reared. Accordingly Gabriel placed his hand upon its mane: then he said, 'O Burâq, art thou not ashamed of what thou

the fact that in Sûrah LIII., An Najm, 13–18, Muḥammad clearly asserts that he saw the *Sidratu'l Muntahâ'*, which stands in the highest heaven. These verses must refer to this *Mi'râj*, and may be thus rendered :—

"And indeed he (Muḥammad) saw him (Gabriel) another time
At the *Sidratu'l Muntahâ'*,
Near it is the Paradise of the Habitation,
When what covered the Lotus-tree covered it :
The gaze (of Muḥammad) glanced not aside nor wandered.
Indeed he saw some of the great signs of his Lord."

art doing? (I swear) by God, O Burâq, there never mounted thee before Muḥammad a servant of God more honoured with God than he is.' Accordingly (Burâq) became so much ashamed that he poured forth sweat. Then he stood still till I mounted him." "Al Ḥasan in his Tradition has said, 'The Apostle of God went, and Gabriel went with him, until he reached the Holy House (Jerusalem) with him. There he found Abraham and Moses and Jesus amid a band of the prophets. Accordingly the Apostle of God acted as their leader (Imâm) in worship, and prayed with them. Thereupon (Gabriel) brought two vessels, in one of which there was wine and in the other milk. Accordingly the Apostle of God took the vessel of milk and drank of it, and left the vessel of wine. Therefore Gabriel said to him, 'Thou hast been guided to Nature and thy people have been guided to Nature, O Muḥammad, and wine is forbidden you.' Then the Apostle of God departed, and when it was morning he went to the Quraish and gave them this information. Then said very many people, 'By God! this matter is clear: by God! a caravan takes a month from Mecca to Syria, and a month in returning, and does that fellow Muḥammad go in one night and come back to Mecca[1]?'"

According to this narrative, Muḥammad went

[1] *Sîratu'r Rasûl*, pp. 138, 139.

only from Mecca to Jerusalem and back in one night. Later traditions amplify the journey considerably, all, however, professing to give the account which the reciter declared came from Muḥammad himself. In the *Mishkâtu'l Maṣâbîḥ* the following story is given, with the usual string of names of those through whom the tradition was handed down:—

"The Prophet[1] of God related, . . . While I was asleep, . . . lo! a comer came to me: then he opened what is between this and this . . ., and he took out my heart. Then I was brought a golden cup full of faith. My heart was washed, then it was replaced, then I came to myself. . . . Then I was brought an animal smaller than a mule and taller than a donkey, and white: it is called Burâq, and places its front feet at the far end of its range of sight. Then I was set upon it, and Gabriel carried me off until I came to the lowest heaven. He demanded admittance. It was said, 'Who is that?' He said, 'Gabriel.' It was said, 'And who is with thee?' He said, 'Muḥammad.' It was said, 'And was he sent for?' He said, 'Yes.' It was said, 'Welcome to him, and very good is his coming.' Then one opened. Accordingly, when I entered, lo! Adam was there. Gabriel said, 'This is thy father Adam, therefore salute him.' Accordingly I saluted

[1] *Mishkât*, pp. 518–20.

him, and he returned the salute. Then he said, 'Welcome to the good son and the good prophet.'" The story goes on with wearisome repetition of much the same account, telling us how Gabriel took Muḥammad from heaven to heaven, being asked the same questions at each door, and answering them in precisely the same way. In the second heaven Muḥammad was introduced to John the Baptist and Jesus, in the third to Joseph, in the fourth to Idrîs, in the fifth to Aaron, in the sixth to Moses. The latter wept, and when asked why, replied that the cause of his tears was the knowledge that more of Muḥammad's followers than of his own people would enter Paradise. In the seventh heaven Muḥammad met Abraham, and the usual greeting took place. "Afterwards I was carried aloft to the *Sidratu'l Muntahâ'* [1], and lo! its fruits were like the pots of a potter, and lo! its leaves were like the ears of an elephant. He said, 'This is the Lotus of the Boundary.' Then lo! four rivers, two interior rivers and two exterior rivers. I said, 'What are these two, O Gabriel?' He said, 'The two interior ones are two rivers in Paradise, but the two exterior ones are the Nile and the Euphrates.'"

The passage goes on to mention many other particulars of the journey, among others the

[1] "The Lotus of the Boundary," so called because even Gabriel must not pass it.

incident of Adam's weeping, which we have[1] already spoken of; but it is unnecessary to mention them all.

In the popular works[2] from which the great mass of modern Muslims obtain their knowledge of their prophet's life, the account of the *Mi'râj* is far more full of marvels. When he had reached the Lotus of the Boundary, beyond which Gabriel dared not advance with him, the angel Isrâfîl took charge of Muḥammad and led him to his own realm, whence the prophet advanced to the very Throne of God, being bidden by God's own Voice not to remove his sandals, since their touch[3] would honour even the court of God. After a few more details, which to ordinary minds seem both puerile and blasphemous, we are told that Muḥammad entered behind the veil[4], and that God said to him, "Peace be upon thee, and the mercy of God, and His blessing, O Prophet." In these later narratives of the *Mi'râj* we find mythology unrestrained by any regard for reason or truth.

We must now inquire what was the source from which the idea of this night journey of Muḥammad was derived. It is very possible that the legend

[1] pp. 206 sqq.

[2] Such as the *Qiṣaṣu'l Anbiyâ*, the *'Arâisu't Tijân*, the *Rauḍatu'l Aḥbâb*, &c.

[3] *Qiṣaṣu'l Anbiyâ*, pp. 337, 338.

[4] Perhaps an invention to make him bear comparison with our Lord: cf. Heb. vi. 19, 20.

as first of all related by Muḥammad himself was based upon a dream, and it does not seem to have contained any account of an ascension, *if* we consider Surah LIII., 13–18, to be of later date. But we have to deal with the narrative contained in the Traditions, and these enter into very precise details regarding the *Mi'râj* or "ascent." We shall see that there is good reason to believe that the legend in this form was invented in order to show that, in this respect as well as in all others, Muḥammad was more highly privileged than any other prophet. The story may have incorporated elements from many quarters, but it seems to have been in the main based upon the account of the ascension of Artâ Vîrâf contained in a Pahlavî book called "The Book [1] of Artâ Vîrâf," which was composed in the days of Ardashîr Bâbagân, King of Persia, some 400 years before Muḥammad's *Hijrah*, if we may believe Zoroastrian accounts.

In that work we are informed that, finding that the Zoroastrian faith had to a great extent lost its hold upon the minds of the people of the Persian Empire, the Magian priests determined to support by fresh proofs the restoration of the faith which the zeal of Ardashîr had undertaken to carry out. Therefore they selected a young priest of saintly life, and prepared him by various ceremonial purifications for an ascent into the heavens, in order that he might see what was there and bring back

[1] *Artâ Virâf Nâmak.*

word whether it agreed or not with the accounts contained in their religious books. It is related that, when this young Artâ Vîrâf was in a trance, his spirit ascended into the heavens under the guidance of an archangel named Sarôsh, and passed from one storey to another, gradually ascending until he reached the presence of Ôrmazd[1] himself. When Artâ Vîrâf had thus beheld everything in the heavens and seen the happy state of their inhabitants, Ôrmazd commanded him to return to the earth as His messenger and to tell the Zoroastrians what he had seen. All his visions are fully related in the book which bears his name. It is unnecessary to quote it at length, but a few quotations will serve to show how evidently it served as a model for the Muḥammadan legend of the ascent of Muḥammad.

In the *Artâ Vîrâf Nâmak* (cap. vii, §§ 1–4) we read: "And I take the first step forward unto the Storey of the Stars, in *Hûmat*. . . . And I see the souls of those holy ones, from whom light spreads out like a bright star. And there is a throne and a seat, very bright and lofty and exalted. Then I inquired of holy Sarôsh and the angel Âdhar, 'What place is this, and who are these persons?'"

In explanation of this passage it should be mentioned that the "Storey of the Stars" is the first or lowest "court" of the Zoroastrian Paradise.

[1] *Ôrmazd* is the later form of the Avestic Ahurâ Mazdâo, the Good God of Zoroastrianism.

Âdhar is the angel who presides over fire. Sarôsh is the angel of obedience, and is one of the "Eternal Holy Ones" (*Amesha-speñtas*, later *Amshâspands*) or archangels of the Zoroastrian faith. He guides Artâ Vîrâf through the different heavens, just as Gabriel does Muḥammad.

The narrative goes on to relate how Artâ Vîrâf reached the Storey of the Moon, or the second, and then the Storey of the Sun, which is the third of the celestial mansions. In the same way he was led on and on through every one of the heavens, until he was introduced into Ôrmazd's presence, and had the interview which is detailed in cap. xi in these words:—

"And finally up rose from his throne overlaid with gold the archangel Bahman: and he took my hand and brought me to Hûmat and Hûkht and Hûrast[1], amid Ôrmazd and the archangels and the other holy ones and the Essence of Zoroaster the pure-minded . . . and the other faithful ones and chiefs of the faith, than whom I have never seen anything brighter and better. And Bahman [said], 'This is Ôrmazd.' And I wished to offer a salutation before Him. And he said to me, 'Salutation to thee, O Artâ Vîrâf! Welcome! Thou hast come from that perishable world to this

[1] Three courts of Paradise, called in the Avestâ *Humata* ("good thought"), *Hûkhta* ("good word") and *Hvarsta* ("good deed"). They correspond to the Star Court (Storey of the Stars), Moon Court, and Sun Court respectively.

undefiled bright place.' And he commanded holy Sarôsh and the angel Âdhar, 'Carry off Artâ Vîrâf and show him the throne and the reward of the holy ones and also the punishment of the wicked.' And finally holy Sarôsh and the angel Âdhar took my hand, and I was carried forward by them from place to place; and I have seen those archangels, and I have seen the other angels."

We are then told at considerable length how Artâ Vîrâf visited Paradise and hell, and what he saw in each. After his visit to hell the tale goes on:—

"At[1] last holy Sarôsh and the angel Âdhar took my hand and brought me forth from that dark, dreadful and terrible place, and they bore me to that place of brightness and the assembly of Ôrmazd and the archangels. Then I wished to offer a salutation before Ôrmazd. And He was kind. He said, 'O faithful servant, holy Artâ Vîrâf, apostle of the worshippers of Ôrmazd, go thou to the material world, speak with truth to the creatures, according as thou hast seen and known, since I, who am Ôrmazd, am here. Whosoever speaks rightly and truly, I hear and know. Speak thou to the wise ones.' And when Ôrmazd spake thus, I remained astounded, for I saw a light and did not see a body, and I heard a voice, and I knew that 'this is Ôrmazd.'"

It is unnecessary to point out how great is the

[1] Cap. ci.

resemblance between all this and the Muḥammadan legend of Muḥammad's *Mi'râj*.

In the *Zardusht-Nâmah*, a work which was probably composed in the thirteenth century of the Christian era, there is related a legend that Zoroaster himself, centuries earlier than Artâ Vîrâf, ascended up to heaven, and afterwards obtained permission to visit hell also. There we are told he saw Ahriman, who closely corresponds with the Iblîs of the Qur'ân.

Nor are such legends confined to the Persian portion of the Âryan world. In Sanskṛit also we have similar tales, among which may be mentioned the *Indralokagamanam*, or "Journey to the World of Indra," the god of the atmosphere. There we are told that the hero Arjuna made a journey through the heavens, where he saw Indra's heavenly palace, named Vaivanti, which stands in the garden called Nandanam. The Hindû books tell us that ever-flowing streams water the fresh, green plants that grow in that beautiful place, and in its midst there stands a tree called Pakshajati, bearing a fruit styled *Amṛita* or Immortality, the ἀμβροσία of Greek poets, of which whoever eats never dies. Beautiful flowers of varied hues adorn that tree; and whoever rests under its shade is granted the fulfilment of whatever desire he may conceive in his heart.

The Zoroastrians have also an account of the existence of a marvellous tree, called *Ḥvâpa* in the

Avestâ and *Hûmayâ* in Pahlavî, the meaning in each case being "possessed of good water," "well watered." In the *Vendîdâd* it is described in these words:—"In[1] purity do the waters flow from the sea of Pûitika into the sea of Vourukasha, to the tree Ḥvâpa: there grow all plants and of all kinds." Ḥvâpa and Pakshajati are identical with the Ṭûbâ' or tree of "goodness" of the Muḥammadan paradise, which is too well known to need description here.

It must, however, be noted that very similar legends are found in certain Christian apocryphal works also, especially in the "Visio Pauli" and the "Testament of Abraham," to the latter of which we have already had to refer more than once. In the "Visio Pauli" we are told that Paul ascended to the heavens and beheld the four rivers of Paradise: and Abraham also viewed the wonders of the heavens in his legendary "Testament," each returning to earth to relate what he had seen, just as Artâ Vîrâf and Muḥammad are said to have done. Of Abraham it is said: "And[2] the archangel Michael descended and took Abraham up upon a cherubic chariot, and he raised him aloft into the ether of the sky, and brought him and sixty angels upon the cloud; and Abraham was travelling over the whole inhabited earth upon a conveyance."

This "cherubic chariot" assumes another form

[1] *Vendîdâd*, cap. v.

[2] "Testament of Abraham," Rec. A., cap. x.

in the Muḥammadan legend, for Muḥammad rides upon an animal called *Burâq*, riding being more in accordance with Arabian ideas than driving. The word *Burâq* is probably derived from the Hebrew *bârâq*, "lightning," which in Arabic is *barq*, though a Pahlavî derivation is also possible.

Before passing on to consider other points, it should be noticed that the Book of Enoch contains a long account of the wonders of earth, hell and sky which Enoch saw in his[1] vision (ὁράσει). This apocryphal work no doubt had its influence on the legends contained in the "Visio Pauli" and the "Testament of Abraham" and thus upon the Muḥammadan fable; but we can hardly suppose that the *Artâ Vîrâf Nâmak* was affected, except perhaps indirectly, by these works. However, that is a question which does not affect our present inquiry.

Now regarding the Tree of Life in the Garden of Eden the Jews have many marvellous[2] legends, which may have been borrowed from the Accadian tales about the "Sacred Tree of Eriṭu," mentioned in some of the earliest inscriptions found at Nippur

[1] Liber Henoch, capp. xiv, xv, sqq.

[2] In the Targum of Jonathan, for example, we are told that the Tree of Life was 500 *years' journey in height!* The Muslims confound this with the Tree of the Knowledge of Good and Evil, which they take to have been the wheat plant. Of it we are told that it presented itself before Adam to tempt him to eat of it. Adam rose to his full height, "500 *years' journey*" to avoid it, but the plant grew and kept on a level with his mouth (*Qiṣaṣu'l Anbiyâ*, p. 17).

by Dr. Hilprecht. Into these we need not now enter at any length, merely observing how great a contrast there is between all such legends and the simple narrative of fact contained in Genesis. The Jewish legends have affected the Muḥammadan account of the heavenly Paradise, because the Muslim belief is that the Garden of Eden was situated in heaven. They therefore transfer to the heavenly Paradise much that the Jews have related about the earthly. In this respect they may have been led into error by the Christian apocryphal books, for the description of the four rivers, &c., given in the "Visio Pauli" (cap. xlv) evidently springs from the same strange fancy. It is hardly necessary to say that these apocryphal books were never accepted by any section of the Christian Church as of any weight or authority, though some of them had at one time a considerable degree of popularity with the ignorant multitude. Some of them have long been known, others have only recently been recovered after having been lost for centuries. Whether the Muḥammadans derived their account of the tree Ṭûbâ' from the Zoroastrians or from Jewish fables, or whether both the latter (being of common origin) have not had some influence on the story, we need not inquire. The four rivers that Muḥammad saw are those of the "Visio Pauli," and these latter are identical with the rivers of Eden, owing to the error which we have noticed above.

It may be asked whether the biblical account of the ascension of Enoch, Elijah, our Lord, and the "catching[1] up to the third heaven" of the person whom some have supposed to be St. Paul, have not been the original sources of all the fables which we have met with[2]. It is somewhat difficult and quite unnecessary to suppose this with reference to the Persian and Indian tales to which we have referred, though it may be true of the others.

[1] 2 Cor. xii. 2–4.

[2] A Muḥammadan might add, "If we reject the account of Muḥammad's ascension, how can we accept those of Enoch, Elijah, and Christ?" The answer is not far to seek. The historical evidence for Christ's ascension is unquestionable, and we accept the other accounts upon His authority. Moreover, to urge that there can be no genuine coins because there are known to be some spurious ones in circulation is not very logical. There would be no spurious ones if there had not been genuine coins, upon the model of which the latter have been made. Hence the very existence of so many legends of ascensions should lead us *a priori* to infer that these must be based upon some one or more true accounts of such occurrences. Moreover, as the true coin may be known from the false by its ring, so a comparison between the biblical narratives (Gen. v. 24; 2 Kings ii. 11, 12; Acts i. 9–11) and those others which we have been dealing with will suffice to show what an immense difference exists between them. For instance, St. Paul tells us of some one who (whether in the body or not he did not know) was "caught up to the third heaven, and heard unspeakable words, which it is not lawful for a man to utter." But the apocryphal "Visio Pauli" states that Paul was the person referred to, and puts in his mouth a long account of what he saw and heard there. The difference is much the same as that which exists between the testimony of a sober historian and the wonderful tales contained in the *Arabian Nights*.

But if it be so, we find that the Muslim legend of Muḥammad's ascent, like so many other legends[1] about Muḥammad, has been invented, on the model of other accounts like that contained in the *Artâ Vîrâf Nâmak*, with the object of making it appear that he was in certain respects similar, though superior, to Christ and the other prophets who preceded him.

2. *The Muḥammadan Paradise with its Ḥûrîs.*

With these we may couple the *Ghilmân*, the *Jinns*, the Angel of Death, and the *Dharrâtu'l Kâinât*.

As examples of the descriptions which the Qur'ân gives of Paradise, we may quote the following passages[2]:—

Sûrah LV., Ar Raḥmân, 46 sqq.: "And for him who feareth the tribunal of his Lord there are two gardens, dowered with branches. In each of them two fountains flow. In each of them there are of every fruit two kinds. They recline upon couches of which the inner lining is of brocade: and the fruit of the two gardens hangs low. In them are [maidens] restraining their glances, whom neither man nor demon hath approached before them. They are as it were rubies and pearls. Is the recompense for kindness other than kindness?

[1] Dr Koelle, *Mohammed and Mohammedanism*, pp. 246 sqq.

[2] Similar passages may be found in Sûrahs II., IV., XIII., XXXVI., XXXVII., XLVII., LXXXIII., &c.

And besides these two there are two [other] gardens, dark green. In each of them are two fountains, flowing abundantly. In each of them are fruits and palms and pomegranates. In each are [maidens] good, beauteous, *Ḥûrîs* enclosed in pavilions, whom neither man nor demon hath approached before them. [The Just] recline on green pillows and beautiful carpets."

Again, in Sûrah LVI., Al Wâqi'ah, 11 sqq., we find a similar account of the delights reserved in Paradise for the "Companions of the Right Hand," —that is, the saved—on the Resurrection Day:— "These are those who are brought nigh, in gardens of delight . . . upon bejewelled couches, reclining upon them, facing one another. Upon them wait immortal youths" (the *Ghilmân*), "with goblets and beakers and a cup from a spring [of wine][1]. They do not suffer headache from it, nor do they become intoxicated. And with fruit of whatever kind they choose, and birds' flesh of whatever sort they desire. And there are large-eyed *Ḥûrîs* like hidden pearls, a recompense for what they used to do. They do not hear in it any vain discourse, nor any charge of crime, only the word 'Peace, Peace.' And the Companions of the Right Hand—what of the Companions of the Right Hand? In a thornless Lotus-tree and a flower-bedecked Acacia and widespread shade and streaming water, and with

[1] Wine is shown to be meant from the context. Rivers of wine are spoken of in Sûrah XLVII., 16.

abundant fruit not cut off and not forbidden, and in raised couches. Verily We have produced them" (these damsels) "by a [peculiar] creation. Therefore have We made them virgins, beloved, of an equal age [with their spouses] for the Companions of the Right Hand[1]."

We shall see that much of this description is derived from Persian and Hindû ideas of Paradise, though most of the more unpleasant details and conceptions are doubtless the offspring of Muḥammad's own sensual nature.

The idea of the *Ḥûrîs* is derived from the ancient Persian legends about the Pairakas, called by the modern people of Îrân *Parîs*. These the Zoroastrians describe as female spirits living in the air and closely connected with the stars and light. So beautiful are they that they captivate men's hearts. The word *Ḥûr*, by which these damsels of Paradise are spoken of in the Qur'ân, is generally supposed to be of Arabic derivation, and to mean "black-eyed." This is quite possible. But it is perhaps more probably a Persian word, derived from the word which in Avestic is *hvare*, in Pahlavî *hûr*, and in modern Persian *khûr*, originally denoting "light," "brightness," "sunshine," and finally "the sun." When the Arabs borrowed the conception of these bright and "sunny" maidens from

[1] Much more graphic pictures of Paradise and its pleasures are given in the Traditions. *Vide* the *Saḥîḥ* of Bukhârî and the *Mishkâtu'l Maṣâbîḥ* on the subject.

the Persians, they also perhaps borrowed the word which best described them. It was natural for the Arabs to find a meaning in their own language for the word, just as in a similar way *asparagus* has become "sparrow-grass," *renegade* "runagate," the *girasole* a "Jerusalem" artichoke, or in Greek the Arabic word *wâdî*, having become Hellenized under the form *ὄασις*, was supposed to come from *αὔω*,—doubtless on the *lucus a non lucendo* principle. *Firdaus* itself, one of the words in the Qur'ân for "Paradise," is a Persian word; and several words from that[1] language occur in the passages which we have translated above. It is not, however, of any real importance to ascertain the derivation of the word *Ḥûr*. The beings whom the word is intended to express are of distinctly Âryan origin, as are the *Ghilmân*. The Hindûs believe in the existence of both, calling the Ḥûrîs in Sanskṛit *Apsarasas*, and the Ghilmân *Gandharvas*. They were supposed to dwell principally in the sky, though often visiting the earth.

Muslim historians relate many tales which show how much the prospect of receiving a welcome from the Ḥûrîs in Paradise cheered many an ardent young Muḥammadan warrior to rush boldly to his death in battle. This belief is very similar to the ancient Âryan idea as to the reward of those who died on the field with all their wounds

[1] See Al Kindî's *Apology*: Sir W. Muir's translation, pp. 79, 80, and notes.

in front. For Manu says in his *Dharmaśâstra*: "Earth-lords[1] contending in battles, mutually desirous of killing one another, not averting their faces, thereafter through their prowess go to heaven." So also in the *Nalopâkhyânam* we find Indra saying to the hero Nala: "Just[2] guardians of the earth (*i.e.* kings), warriors who have abandoned (all hope of) life, who in due time by means of a weapon go to destruction without averting their faces—theirs is this imperishable world"—the heaven of Indra. Nor were such ideas confined to India, for our own northern ancestors used in heathen days to believe that the heavenly Valkyries, or "Selectors of the Slain," would visit[3] the field of battle and bear thence to the heaven of Odhin, to Valhalla, the "Hall of the Slain," the spirits of brave warriors who fell in the strife.

The *Jinns* are a kind of evil and malicious spirits which have great power and are a source of terror in many parts of the Muslim world. We have already seen[4] that they are said to have been subject to Solomon, and they are not unfrequently

[1] "Âhaveshumitho 'nyo 'nyam jighaṃsanto mahîkshita*h*
Yudhyamânâ*h* paraṃšaktyâsvargam yântyaparâ*n*mukhâ*h*."
—*Dharmašâstra*, bk. vii, šl. 89.

[2] "Dharmajñâ*h* pṛithivîpâlâs tyaktajîvitayodhina*h*
Šastreṇa nidhanam kâle ye gacchantyaparâ*n*mukhâ*h*
Ayam loko 'kshayas teshâm."—*Nalopákhyânam* ii. 17, 18.

[3] Cf. the Armenian Aṛalêzk'h (Ezniq Goghbatsi, 'Eghds Aghandots,' bk. i., pp. 94, 95).

[4] pp. 81 sqq.

mentioned in the Qur'ân[1], where we are told that they were made of fire[2], as were the angels and the demons. The word itself seems to be Persian, for the singular *Jinní* is the Avestic *Jaini*[3], a wicked (female) spirit.

In examining the question of the origin of the Muḥammadan legend regarding the "Balance," we saw that it is stated in the Traditions that in his *Mi'râj* Muḥammad saw Adam weeping in heaven when he looked at[4] the "Black Figures" (*al aswidah*) on his left hand, but rejoicing when his glance rested on those which stood at his right.

These black figures were the spirits of his descendants *as yet unborn.* They are generally termed "The Existent Atoms" (*adh dharrâtu'l kâinât*). They differ from the beings mentioned in the "Testament of Abraham" (from which the main features of that portion of the tale are borrowed) in the fact that, in the latter book, Abraham sees the spirits of his descendants *who had died*, while in the Muḥammadan tradition he sees those of men *not yet born*, in the form of "Existent Atoms." The name by which these beings are known in Muḥammadan religious works

[1] Sûrahs VI., 100, 128 ; XV., 27 ; XXVI., 212 ; XLI., 24, 29, &c.

[2] Sûrahs XV., 27 ; LV., 14.

[3] *Yasna*, X., § 4 : 2, 53. If the word were Arabic and from the root جَنّ, it would be not *jinní* but *janín* (like *qalíl* from قَلّ). Nor is it derived from *jannat*, Paradise, for then it would be *jannī*. Moreover, the *Jinns* have no connexion with Paradise, and are not allowed to enter it.

[4] pp. 207, 208.

is undoubtedly a purely Arabic one. But the *idea* seems to have been derived from the Zoroastrians, among whom these beings were called *fravashis*[1] in Avestic and *ferûhars* in Pahlavî. Some have fancied that possibly the Persians adopted this idea from the ancient Egyptians, but this hardly seems probable. Whether it be so or not, the Muslims are indebted for their belief in the pre-existence of men's spirits to the Zoroastrians.

The Muslims speak of the Angel of Death very much as the Jews do, though the latter say that his name is Sammâêl, while the former call him 'Azrâîl. But this latter name is not Arabic but *Hebrew*, once more showing the extent of the influence exercised by the Jews upon nascent Islâm. As this angel's name is not mentioned in the Bible, it is evident that what the Jews and the Muslims say about him must be borrowed from some other source. This is probably Persian, for the Avestâ tells us of an angel called *Astô-vîdhôtuš* or *Vîdhâtuš*, "the divider," whose duty it is to separate body and spirit. If a man fell into fire or water and was burnt to death or drowned, the Zoroastrians held that his death could not be due to the fire or to the water—for

[1] The *Fravashis* are both spiritual prototypes and guardian angels, protecting Ôrmazd's creatures. Every such being, whether born or unborn, has a *fravashi*, as have even Ôrmazd, the Amshâspands and the Îzads. The "Grandson of the Waters," the genius who presides over fertility and fecundity, brings the *fravashis* to their bodies in *Yesht* VIII., 34.

these "elements" were supposed to be good and not injurious to man. It was the work of the Angel of Death, Vîdhâtuš[1].

3. *The Ascent of 'Azâzîl from Hell.*

'Azâzîl, according to the Muslim tradition, was the original name of Satan or Iblîs. The name is Hebrew and occurs in the original text of Leviticus (xvi. 8, 10, 26). But the tale of his origin is not at all Jewish but almost if not quite Zoroastrian, as a comparison between the Muslim and the Zoroastrian legends proves.

In the *Qiṣaṣu'l Anbiyâ* (p. 9), we read: "God Most High created 'Azâzîl. 'Azâzîl worshipped God Most High for a thousand years in *Sijjîn*[2]. Then he came up to the earth. On each story[3] he worshipped God Most High for a thousand years until he came up upon the surface," the highest story, on which men dwell. God then gave him a pair of wings made of emerald, with which he mounted up to the first heaven. There he worshipped for a thousand years, and thus was enabled to reach the second heaven, and so on, worshipping for a thousand years at each stage

[1] *Vendidâd*, cap. v, lines 25 to 35.

[2] Or the "Dungeon." This is the name of the seventh or lowest story in hell, and of the book kept there, in which the demons write the evil deeds of apostates and infidels (Sûrah LXXXIII., 7-10).

[3] As has been already said, the earth, like hell and heaven, consists of seven stories.

of his ascent, and receiving from the angelic inhabitants of each heaven a special name. In the fifth heaven he was for the first time—according to this form of the legend—called 'Azâzîl. He thus ascended to the sixth and the seventh heaven, and then had performed so much adoration that he had not left in earth or heaven a single spot as large as the palm of a man's hand on which he had not prostrated himself in worship. Afterwards we are told that for the sin of refusing to worship Adam he was cast out of Paradise[1]. The *'Arâisu'l Majâlis*[2] tells us that, being then called Iblîs, he remained for three thousand years at the gate of Paradise in the hope of being able to inflict some injury on Adam and Eve, since his heart was full of envy and ill-will towards them.

Now let us see what account the Zoroastrians give of what is evidently the same matter in the *Bûndahishnîh*, a Pahlavî work the name of which means "Creation." It must be noted that in Pahlavî the Evil Spirit is called *Ahriman*, which is derived from *Añrô Mainyuš* ("the destroying mind"), the name by which he is known in the Avestâ.

In the first and second chapters of the *Bûndahishnîh* we read:—

"Ahriman was and is in darkness and after-

[1] *Qiṣaṣu'l Anbiyâ*, p. 12 : see above, p. 195.

[2] *'Arâisu'l Majâlis*, p. 43.

knowledge[1] and the desire of inflicting injury, and in the abyss. . . . And that injuriousness and that darkness too are a place which they call the dark region. Ôrmazd in his omniscience knew that Ahriman existed, because he"—that is, Ahriman—"excites himself and intermingles himself with the desire of envy even unto the end. . . . They" (Ôrmazd and Ahriman) "were for three thousand years in spirit, that is, they were without change and motion. . . . The injurious spirit, on account of his after-knowledge, was not aware of the existence of Ôrmazd. At last he rises from that abyss, and he came to the bright place; and, since he saw that brightness of Ôrmazd, . . . because of his injurious desire and his envious disposition he became busied in destroying."

We necessarily find a certain difference in form between the legend as it arose among the dualistic Zoroastrians and the aspect it assumed among the Monotheistic Muslims. Hence in the former the Evil Principle is not a creature of Ôrmazd, and does not at first know of His existence, whereas in the latter he is, of course, one of the creatures of God. In the Muḥammadan legend he gradually ascends higher and higher by his piety, while in the Zoroastrian account piety can have nothing

[1] That is, Ahriman does not know the future but only the past. His *after-knowledge* is the ἐπιμήθεια of the Greeks (Prometheus contrasted with Epimetheus), and Ôrmazd ultimately vanquishes him because the latter alone has foreknowledge.

to do with the matter. But in both cases the Evil Spirit at first dwells in darkness and ignorance and comes up to the light, and in both cases he sets himself to work to destroy God's creatures through envy and ill-will. The twelve thousand years during which, according to Zoroastrian ideas, the contest between good and evil goes on is divided into four periods of three thousand years each. A reference to this is probably to be found in the three thousand years during which, as we have seen, 'Azâzîl (Iblîs) lies in wait for Adam's destruction.

Before leaving this subject it may be of interest to point out that the *Peacock* has some connexion with the Evil Spirit both in the Muḥammadan and in the Zoroastrian legend. In the *Qiṣaṣu'l Anbiyâ* we are told that when Iblîs was seated in ambush before the gate of Paradise, watching for an opportunity to enter and tempt Adam and Eve to sin, the Peacock was sitting on the wall, on top of one of the battlements, and saw him most piously engaged in repeating the loftiest names of God Most High. Struck with admiration for so much piety, the Peacock inquired who this ardent devotee might be. Iblîs replied, "I am one of the angels of God; may He be honoured and glorified!" When asked why he sat there, he replied, "I am looking at Paradise, and I wish to enter it." The Peacock was acting as watchman, so he replied, "I have no orders to admit any one to Paradise while Adam is in it." But Iblîs bribed him to grant him admission by promising to teach him a prayer, the repetition of which would keep him from ever growing old, from rebelling against God, and from ever being driven forth from Paradise. On this the Peacock flew down from the battlement and told the Serpent what he had heard. This led to the fall of Eve and afterwards of Adam. When, therefore, God Most High cast Adam, Eve, the Tempter and the Serpent down from Paradise to the earth, he hurled down the Peacock[1] with them.

It is noteworthy that the Zoroastrians also believed in a connexion between Ahriman and the Peacock. The Armenian writer Ezniq, whom we have already quoted in a different connexion, informs us of the Zoroastrians of his day that "They[2] say that Ahriman said, 'It is not that I cannot make anything good, but I will not.' And, in order to prove what he said, he made the Peacock."

If the Peacock in the Zoroastrian legend is a creature of Ahriman, we are not surprised at its helping Iblîs in the Muḥammadan one, and being expelled from Paradise along with him.

4. *Legend of the "Light of Muḥammad."*

Though not mentioned in the Qur'ân, the story of the Light of Muḥammad, which shone on his

[1] *Qiṣaṣu'l Anbiyâ*, pp. 16, 17.

[2] *Refutation of Heresies*, Book ii.

forehead and was his pre-existent essence, so to speak, occupies a very important place in the Traditions. Whole pages are filled with such traditions in such books as the *Rauḍatu'l Aḥbâb*. There we read that "When Adam was created, God placed that light upon his forehead, and said, 'O Adam, this light which I have placed upon thy forehead is the light of the noblest and best son [of thine], and it is the light of the chief of the prophets who shall be sent.'" Then the narrative goes on to say that the light passed on from Adam to Seth, and from Seth to the noblest of his descendants in each generation, until in due course it reached 'Abdu'llâh ibn Al Muṭṭalab. From him it passed to Âminah when she conceived Muḥammad[1]. It may be that Muḥammadans have intended in their account of this light of Muḥammad to exalt their master so as to match what is said of

[1] Another tradition mentions the following facts which are of interest as showing the importance of this light. Muḥammad said, "God Most High divided that light" (before the creation of the world, for "The first thing that he created was my Light," *Qiṣaṣu'l Anbiyâ*, p. 2, vide also p. 282) "into four sections, and He created the Throne" (or Highest Heaven, *Al 'Arsh*) "out of one section, and from one section He created the Pen, and from one section He created Paradise, and from one section He created the Believers. He again divided these four sections into four other parts. Out of the first, the choicest and most honourable, He created me, who am the Apostle, and from the second part He created Reason and placed it in the Believers' head, and out of the third part He created modesty and placed it in Believers' eyes, and out of the fourth part He created Desire, and placed it in Believers' hearts." (*Qiṣaṣu'l Anbiyâ*, p. 2.)

Christ in John i. 4, 5 (cf. xii. 41), and that there is a confusion in their minds between the first of these passages and Gen. i. 3. At the same time it will be seen from the passages which we now proceed to quote that the details, though with marvellous exaggeration and invention, are, in their main outline, borrowed from Zoroastrian legend.

In the Pahlavî *Mînûkhirad*, which was composed in the days of the early Sâsânian kings of Persia, we read that Ôrmazd created this world and all His creatures, and the archangels, and the Heavenly Reason, out of His own special light, with the praise of *Zarvân i Akarana* or "Endless Time." But in a work far more ancient than this the fable of the light is found existent in Persia. In the Avestâ it is mentioned in connexion with the great Yima *Khshaêta* or Yima "the Brilliant," who from its possession derived his name, afterwards corrupted into the modern Persian Jamshîd. He is identical with the Sanskrit *Yama*, who in the Rig Veda is spoken of as the first of men, as in vain tempted to sin by his twin sister Yamî, and as after death ruling the shades of the dead. Yima, in Persian tradition on the other hand, is the founder of Persian civilization. His father's name, Vîvaṅhvat[1], is the same as the Vivasvat of the Indian legend, who is the Sun, and is father

[1] In Persian legend, Vîvaṅhvat is the fifth in descent from Gaya Maretan, the first man (*Yasna*, IX., 4).

of Yama. On Yima's brow shone the *Karaem Hvareno* or "Royal Brightness," an emanation from the Divine glory, until through sin he lost it. Of this the following description is given in the[1] Avestâ:—

"The mighty Royal Brightness for a long time adhered to Jamshîd, master of the good herd, while he reigned on the seven-climed earth, over *dîvs* and men, magicians and Parîs, evil spirits and soothsayers and wizards. . . . Then, when he conceived in mind that false and worthless word, the visible brightness departed from him in the form of a bird. . . . He who is Jamshîd, master of the good herd, Jam, no longer seeing that brightness, became sorrowful; and he, having become troubled, engaged in working hostility upon earth. The first time that brightness departed, that brightness [departed] from Jamshîd, that brightness departed from Jam, son of Vîvañhvat, like[2] a fluttering bird. . . . Mithra took that brightness. When the second time that brightness departed from Jamshîd, that brightness (departed) from Jam, son of Vîvañhvat, it went away like a fluttering bird: Farîdûn, offspring of the Âthwiyânî tribe, the brave tribe, took that brightness, since he was the most victorious man among victorious men. . . . When the third time that brightness departed from Jamshîd, that brightness departed from Jam,

[1] *Yesht*, XIX., 31–38.

[2] Literally, "in the form of."

son of Vîvañhvat, like a fluttering bird: Keresâspa the manly took that brightness, since he was the mightiest among mighty men."

Here we see that, just as in the Muḥammadan legend, the light passes on from generation to generation, to the most worthy man in each. It was natural for the offspring of the Sun to possess this light in the first place, and its transmission marked the handing down of the sovereignty. There seems no special suitability in the legend that it was handed down from Adam to Muḥammad, unless to magnify the prophet in the same way in which the ancient legend glorified these various old Persian heroes.

Moreover, we notice that Jamshîd ruled "over *dîvs* and men, magicians and Parîs, evil spirits and soothsayers and wizards," just as the Jewish and Muḥammadan legends spoken of in an earlier chapter[1] represent Solomon as doing. Doubtless the Jews borrowed this story from the Zoroastrians and passed it on to the Muslims, as we have said in Chapter III.

What the Muslim Tradition says of the dividing up of the "Light of Muḥammad," when first created, into various parts, out of which other things were made, is very similar to the story concerning Zoroaster in the old Persian book entitled ***Dasâtîr i Âsmânî*** whence it was very possibly

[1] pp. 81, 84, and 90, note.

derived, especially as the same idea is found also in older Zoroastrian writings, as in the *Mînûkhirad* quoted above.

5. *The Bridge of the Dead.*

This is called in the Muhammadan Traditions Aṣ-Ṣirâṭ or "The Way." There are many details given about this marvellous bridge, which is said to be finer than a hair and sharper than a sword. It stretches right over the abyss of hell, and is the only way of passing from earth to heaven on the Judgment Day. All will be commanded to cross it. The pious Muslim will do so without difficulty, guided by the angels; but the unbeliever, unable to cross, will fall headlong into hell fire.

Though the word *Ṣirâṭ* is used in the Qur'ân in the metaphorical sense of a *way*, as in the phrase *Aṣ Ṣirâṭu'l Mustaqîm* ("the Right Way," Sûrah I., Al Fâtiḥah, *et passim*), yet it is not properly an Arabic word at all. Its derivation shows the origin of the legend about the bridge of that name. The word comes from no Arabic or indeed Semitic root, but is the Persian *Chinvaṭ* in Arabic letters, since the Arabic language, not having any character to represent the sound *ch* (as in *church*), replaces it by the letter ص (*ṣ*), the first letter in *Ṣirâṭ*. *Chinvaṭ* in Persian means a collector, one that sums up or assembles (*cf.* Sanskṛit √चि) or takes account. Hence it is only by contraction that the Arabic

Ṣirâṭ gets its meaning, for the Avestâ speaks, not of *Chinvaṭ*[1] but of *Chinvatô-peretuš*, "The bridge of him that reckons up" good deeds and bad. This bridge extends from Mount Alburz to the Chakât Dâitih, reaching over hell. Each man's spirit, as soon as certain funeral ceremonies have been performed, reaches the bridge and has to cross it in order to enter Paradise. When he has crossed the bridge, he is judged by Mithra, Rashnu, and Sraosha in accordance with the account of his deeds, good and bad[2]. Only if his good deeds exceed his evil ones can the gate of Paradise be opened to admit him. If his deeds are preponderatingly evil, he is cast into hell: but if the good are equal to the bad, the spirit of the dead has to await[3] the last judgment (*vîdâiti*), which will take place at the close of the final struggle between Ôrmazd and Ahriman.

To show the origin not only of the word *Ṣirâṭ* but of the Muḥammadan doctrine on the subject, it is sufficient to translate the following short passage from the Pahlavî book called the *Dînkart*:—"I flee[4] from much sin, and I keep pure my conduct by keeping pure the six powers of life—act and speech and thought and intellect and mind

[1] Later, however, the contraction is found in the Zoroastrian books.

[2] See note p. 205 above.

[3] In a place called *Misvânô Gâtuš* (*Vendîdâd*, XIX., 36; *Yesht*, I., 1; *Sîrôzâ*, I., 30; II., 30). Vide above, pp. 123, 124, 202.

[4] *Dînkart*, pt. II., cap. LXXXI., §§ 5 and 6.

and understanding—by thy desire, O mighty Causer of good deeds. In justice do I perform it, that worship of thine, in good thought and speech and deed, in order that I may remain in the bright way, that I may not arrive at the severe punishment of hell, but may cross over Chinvaṭ and may attain to that blessed abode which is full of perfume, wholly pleasant, always brilliant." In the Avestâ also we find many references to the same belief, among others the passage in which it is said of good men and women: "Whom[1] too I shall lead through the prayer of such as you: with all blessings shall I guide them to the bridge of Chinvaṭ."

A further proof of the Âryan origin of this belief is found in the fact that the ancient Scandinavian mythology contains mention of *Bifrǫst*, generally styled "the bridge of the gods," by which they cross over from their abode in *Âsgardh* (in heaven) to the earth. It is the rainbow. This at once explains the natural basis upon which the legend of the bridge is founded, and shows how ancient it is, as the Scandinavians brought the idea with them to Europe. It must therefore have been common to them and the Persians in very ancient times. In Greece the rainbow becomes the messenger of the gods (Iris) in the Iliad, but the idea of a bridge connecting heaven and earth seems to have been lost.

[1] *Yasna*, XLVI., 10.

6. *Other Persian Ideas Borrowed.*

There are, no doubt, many other matters in which Persian ideas have influenced Islâm, but what has been said is sufficient for our purpose. We must not conclude this part of our inquiry, however, without a reference to two other points of some little importance.

One of these is the Muslim belief that every prophet before his death gave notice of the coming of his successor. This idea finds no support in the Bible, where we find prophecies of the coming of the Messiah, but nothing to give rise to the Muhammadan theory. It is probably borrowed from a Zoroastrian work called the *Dasâtîr i Âsmânî*. This work claims to be of very great antiquity, and (owing doubtless to the difficulty of making any sense out of the original[1] text) is believed by many of the modern Pârsîs to be "composed in the language of heaven"! An interlinear translation into the old Darî dialect of Persian, however, accompanies the text, which is said to have been discovered in Persia early in the last century,

[1] The original text (as published in Bombay) is written in Arabic (Persian) characters. By retranslating the Darî in a few passages into Pahlavî and then writing the latter in Arabic characters, I think I have proved that the difficulty in understanding the original text consists in the fact that the transcriber into the Arabic character did not know Pahlavî, and confounded with one another the very difficult combinations of letters in that confused current script.

and was edited by Mullâ Fîrûz of Bombay. It consists of fifteen tractates which are supposed to have been revealed to fifteen successive prophets, the first of whom is styled Mahâbâd and the last Sâsân, from whom probably the Sâsânian dynasty may be supposed to trace their descent. The Darî translation is said to date from the time of Khusrau Parvîz (A.D. 590–5), so that the original must be of some antiquity[1]. Near the conclusion of each tractate but the last there is what purports to be a prophecy of the coming of the next prophet in succession. The object of this is very evident. Many Pârsîs reject the book, but the idea seems to have pleased the Muslims so much that it has found an entrance into their ordinary belief.

Secondly, it is worthy of note that the *second* verse of every one of these tractates runs thus: "In the name of God, the Giver, the Forgiver, the Merciful, the Just." It is evident that these words are closely related to those which form the introduction to every Sûrah of the Qur'ân except the ninth: "In the Name of God, the Compassionate, the Merciful." Probably the Qur'ân has borrowed from the Zoroastrian book and not conversely: for the *Bûndahishnîh* has the similar clause, "In the Name of Ôrmazd the Creator."

[1] It is mentioned by the authors of the *Dabistân i Mazâhib* and of the *Burhân i Qâṭi'*, so it must have been lost since their day. We have mentioned its recovery.

Others think that the clause in the Qur'ân is of Jewish origin. Tradition says that one of the *Ḥanîfs*, whom we shall deal with in our next chapter, Ummiyyah, a poet belonging to Ṭâif, taught this formula to the Quraish [1], having learnt it from his intercourse with Jews and Christians during his journeys in Syria and elsewhere as a merchant. If Muḥammad heard it in this way and adopted it, he doubtless altered it somewhat, as he always did whatever he borrowed. But it is more probably of Zoroastrian origin than of Jewish, and Ummiyyah might have learnt it from the Persians whom he met on his mercantile expeditions.

We have seen how extensive Persian influence was in Arabia in Muḥammad's time, and there is therefore no *a priori* difficulty in accepting the conclusion which must be drawn from all the coincidences mentioned in the present chapter—that Zoroastrian ideas and legends are one of the sources from which Islâm has derived very much of what is contained in certain parts of the Qur'ân and the Traditions. Tradition itself proves the possibility of this, for the *Rauḍatu'l Aḥbâb* tells us that it was Muḥammad's habit to speak [2] a few

[1] *Kitâbu'l Aghânî*, 16 (quoted by Rodwell, *Koran*, p. 1).

[2] In the *Sunan* of Ibn Mâjah a tradition is found on the authority of Abû Hurairah, who says that Muḥammad said to him in Persian, *Shikamat dard?* His knowledge of the language

words in their own language to people that came to him from different nations, and that, since on one or two occasions he spoke Persian to such visitors, a few Persian words in this way found an entrance into the Arabic language. Of course there is a good deal of the legendary in this statement, but it is important in its way because it clearly testifies to the fact that Muḥammad had at least some slight acquaintance with Persian, if with no other foreign tongue. Again, among other Persian converts, the *Sîratu'r Rasûl* of Ibn Isḥâq and Ibn Hishâm informs us that there was one called Salmân, who must have been a man of some education and ability, since it was by his advice and in accordance with his military experience that Muḥammad, when the Quraish and their allies were besieging Medina in February, A.D. 627, defended the city with the celebrated ditch [1], a method of fortification which the Arabs are said not to have previously used. By Salmân's advice Muḥammad is also said to have used a catapult at the time of his campaign against Ṭâif (A.D. 630). Some say that Salmân, though always known as "the Persian," was originally a Christian [2] carried

failed to supply the verb *mîkunad*, which is required to complete the sense.

[1] The Persian word *Kandak* (now *Kandah*) has been adopted into Arabic, and occurs in the *Sîrat* in the form *Khandaq*.

[2] Other accounts say he was first a Zoroastrian, being a Persian by birth; he then became a Christian and went to Syria, from which country he was brought to Arabia.

away captive from Mesopotamia. This may or may not be true, though the appellation which he received does not support it. If it is *untrue*, he was very probably the person whom Muḥammad's enemies are said to have accused the Prophet of using as his assistant in the composition of certain parts of the Qur'ân; for in Sûrah XVI., An Naḥl, 105, we read: "Truly we know that they say, 'Verily a human being teacheth him.' The tongue of him at whom they aim is Persian[1], and this [book] is Arabic, clear." If Salmân was not a native of Persia, then the language of the verse suffices to prove that there *was* some Persian in Muḥammad's company who was believed to "teach" him a certain portion of what he was then inserting in the Qur'ân. We see then that Persian fables were well enough known[2] in Arabia to be recognized by some at least of the Arabs when incorporated into the supposed Divine Revelation. Nor was Muḥammad able to give a satisfactory answer to the charge, for no one supposed that the foreigner was teaching him to improve his Arabic style. The charge affected the matter and not the language of the Qur'ân. Moreover, as we have proved that Muḥammad borrowed legends from the heathen Arabs and from the Jews, there is no reason why he should not be ready and willing to

[1] The word *'Ajami* properly means *Persian*, though capable of being applied to other foreigners.

[2] Vide pp. 215, 216, 217.

adopt others from Zoroastrian sources. In fact the instances which we have produced in this chapter prove conclusively that he did so, and that these Persian legends, many of which have been shown to be common to the Persians with other branches of the Âryan family of nations, form another of the original sources of Islâm.

CHAPTER VI.

THE *ḤANÎFS* AND THEIR INFLUENCE UPON NASCENT ISLÂM. CONCLUSION.

MUḤAMMAD was by no means the first of his nation who became convinced of the folly and worthlessness of the popular religion of the Arabs of the time, and desired to effect a reform. Some years before his appearance as a Prophet, as we learn from his earliest extant biographers, a number of men arose in Medina, Ṭâif, and Mecca, and perhaps in other places[1], who rejected the idol-worship and polytheism of the people at large and endeavoured to find the true religion. Whether the first impulse came from the Jews, as is very probable, or from some other quarter, the men of whom we speak determined to restore the worship of God Most High (Allâh Ta'âla') to its proper place by abolishing, not only the cult of the inferior deities who had almost entirely supplanted Him, but also many of the most immoral of the practices then prevalent, opposed as they were to the human conscience and to humanity itself. Whether

[1] Besides the authorities mentioned further on, see an interesting story about Abû Dharr, related by Muslim in his *Kitábu'l Faḍáil.*

through the survival of a tradition that Abraham, whom they claimed as their ancestor, had known and worshipped the One True God, or through the statement of the Jews to that effect, these reformers asserted that they were seeking for the "Religion of Abraham." It may have been Jewish exclusiveness which prevented them from accepting the faith of these latter in the form which it had then assumed, and joining the synagogue. Or, on the other hand, national and family pride may have rendered them unwilling to accept the religion of foreign settlers in their country. It is also possible that some of these reformers may have been able to perceive that the Jewish religion of the time was by no means free from gross superstitions; and the fact that the Christians accused the Jews of having rejected and slain their Messiah, and pointed to their fallen condition as a proof of God's wrath against them, would also have some influence in preventing these more enlightened Arabs from accepting Talmudic Judaism. Whatever the cause may have been, the fact is that the reformers came forth in the first instance as inquirers and not as Jewish or Christian proselytes. The chief of them who are known to us by name are Abû Amîr at Medina, Ummiyyah ibn Zalṭ at Ṭâif, and at Mecca Waraqah, 'Ubaidu'llâh, 'Uthmân and Zaid ibn 'Amr. Others[1] doubtless

[1] History mentions twelve of Muḥammad's 'Companions' who at first were Ḥanîfs.

more or less sympathized with these men, though they commanded no very extensive following.

As these reformers have left us no written record of their beliefs, except one poem which we shall have to consider in due course, it may be of importance to state what authority we have for the statements which we shall make regarding them. Our chief and practically our only authority[1] is the earliest biographer of Muḥammad whose work has come down to us, Ibn Hishâm. The first writer known to us by name who composed an account of Muḥammad's life was Zuhrî, who died in the year 124 of the Hijrah. His information was drawn from what was handed down orally by those who had personally known Muḥammad, and especially by 'Urwah, one of 'Âyishah's kindred. In many respects, doubtless, errors and exaggerations may, during the course of years, have crept into such Traditions; yet if Zuhrî's book were now extant it would be of very great value indeed. But unfortunately it has not been preserved, unless indeed (as is very probable) Ibn Isḥâq, one of Zuhrî's disciples, who died A.H. 151, made use of it in the composition of his own work on Muḥammad's life. Doubtless, however, Ibn Isḥâq added much information which he had collected from other traditional sources, true or false. But even Ibn Isḥâq's book has not come

[1] Sprenger, however, quotes others which he thinks worthy of credence.

down to us in a complete and independent form, though much of it is preserved in the numerous quotations made from it by Ibn Hishâm (died A. H. 213) in his *Sîratu'r Rasûl* or "Biography of the Apostle," the most ancient which we possess of a large number of works which bear the same title. This book is of great value in all matters connected with Muḥammad and his times, for it is evidently far less legendary and fabulous than all other works on the subject.

What Ibn Isḥâq and Ibn Hishâm tell us about the Arabian reformers in particular is worthy of the more credit on this account, because they had no interest in praising them or in exaggerating the resemblance between their teaching and that of Muḥammad. It does not seem to have occurred to these writers that any use could be made of their statements by adversaries, and hence they seem to have told the truth as far as they knew it. It is quite possible that the resemblance between their doctrines and those which Muḥammad promulgated may have been *greater* than the information at our disposal enables us to show, but it can hardly have been less, for the reason we have stated. We may therefore safely rely upon Ibn Hishâm's account as containing at least a minimum of what they taught, and compare it with the Qur'ân.

In order to enable our readers to judge for themselves, we here give a translation of Ibn

Hishâm's narrative, which, it will be noticed, is for the most part founded upon the earlier account given by Ibn Isḥâq.

"Ibn Isḥâq says: And[1] the Quraish assembled one day, at a festival which they had, unto one of their idols which they used to magnify, and to which they used to offer sacrifice, and near which they were wont to remain, and around which they were wont to circle. And that was a festival which they kept one day in every year. Therefore four men secretly kept apart from them. Then said they one to another, 'Be ye true to one another, and let one of you keep another's secret.' They said, 'Very good.' They were Waraqah ibn Asad[2] . . . and 'Ubaidu'llâh ibn Jaḥsh[2] . . ., whose mother was Umaimah, daughter of 'Abdu'l Muṭṭalab, and 'Uthmân ibnu'l Ḥuwairith[2] . . ., and Zaid ibn 'Amr[2] . . . They accordingly said one to another, 'By God, ye know that your nation is based upon nothing: truly they have erred from the religion of their father Abraham. What is a stone[3] that we should circle round it? It hears not, nor sees, nor injures, nor benefits. O people, seek for yourselves [a faith]; for verily, by God, ye are based upon nothing.' Accordingly they went into different lands that they might seek *Ḥanîfism*, the

[1] *Sîratu'r Rasûl*, vol. i, pp. 76, 77.

[2] Here I omit the genealogies, which are given for many generations back.

[3] Referring to the celebrated *Ḥajaru'l Aswad*.

Religion of Abraham. Waraqah ibn Naufal therefore became absorbed in Christianity, and he inquired after the Books among those who professed it, until he acquired some knowledge from the People of the Book. But 'Ubaidu'llâh ibn Jaḥsh remained in the state of uncertainty in which he was until he became a Muslim. He then migrated with the Muslims to Abyssinia, and with him his wife Umm Ḥabîbah, daughter of Abû Sufyân, being a Muslim. When therefore he arrived there, he became a Christian and abandoned Islâm, so that he perished there a Christian. Ibn Isḥâq says: Accordingly Muḥammad ibn Ja'far ibn Zubair has related to me, saying: 'Ubaidu'llâh ibn Jaḥsh, when he became a Christian, used to dispute with the Companions of the Apostle of God who were there in Abyssinia, and he used to say, 'We see clearly and you are blinking,' that is, 'We are clear-sighted and you are seeking to see and do not yet see,' and that because a whelp blinks when it strives to open its eyes to see. The word he used means to have one's eyes open. Ibn Isḥâq says: The Apostle of God succeeded him as husband of Umm Ḥabîbah, daughter of Abû Sufyân ibn Ḥarb. Ibn Isḥâq says: Muḥammad ibn 'Alî ibn Ḥusain has informed me that the Apostle of God sent 'Amr ibn Ummiyah aḍ Ḍamrî to the Negus for her: therefore the Negus betrothed her to him. Accordingly he married him to her. And he fixed as her dowry from the

Apostle of God four hundred dînârs. . . . Ibn Isḥâq says: But 'Uthmân ibn Ḥuwairith went to Caesar, Emperor of Byzantium: then he became a Christian, and his abiding with him prospered. . . Ibn Isḥâq says: But as for Zaid ibn 'Amr ibn Nufail, he remained, and did not enter into Judaism or into Christianity: and he abandoned the religion of his people; therefore he kept aloof from the idols and from carrion and from blood and from the sacrifices which were offered unto the idols, and he forbade the slaughter of infant girls, and he said, 'I serve the Lord of Abraham'; and he reproved his nation for the faults in which they persisted. Ibn Isḥâq says: Hishâm ibn 'Urwah has related to me on the authority of his father, on the authority of *his* mother Asmâ, daughter of Abû Bakr, that she said, 'Truly I saw Zaid ibn 'Amr ibn Nufail as a very old man leaning his back against the Ka'bah and saying, 'O tribe of the Quraish, by Him in whose hand is the soul of Zaid ibn 'Amr, not one of you has attained unto the Religion of Abraham except myself.' Then he would say, 'O God, if I knew which manner is most pleasing to Thee, I should worship Thee in it; but I know it not.' Then he used to worship at his ease[1]. Ibn Isḥâq says: And it is related that his son, Su'aid ibn Zaid ibn 'Amr ibn Nufail, and 'Umar bnu'l Khaṭṭâb, who was his cousin

[1] *Or*, He used to prostrate himself on the palms of his hands.

said to the Apostle of God, 'Pray for forgiveness on behalf of Zaid ibn 'Amr.' He said, 'Yes, for verily he shall be raised up by himself as a religious sect.' Zaid ibn 'Amr ibn Nufail spoke thus in reference to his abandoning the religion of his people and what happened to him from them in consequence:

"One Lord or a thousand Lords
Shall I worship? Are things then partitioned out?
I have abandoned Allât and 'Uzza' altogether:
Thus doeth the hardy, the patient man.
Therefore I worship neither 'Uzza' nor her two daughters,
Nor do I resort unto the two idols of the Banû 'Amr.
Nor do I worship Ghanam, though he was a Lord to us
At the time when my intellect wandered.
I marvelled: both during the nights are there marvellous things
And during the days, which he that seeth clearly understandeth.
For God hath often destroyed men,
Whose condition was immorality.
And others hath he preserved by proving a nation:
Therefore doth He rear up from them the little child.
And among us a man stumbleth: one day he recovereth,
As the branch that drinketh rain is refreshed.
But I serve as my Lord the Merciful One,
That the forgiving Lord may forgive my sin.
Preserve ye therefore the fear of God, your Lord
When ye preserve it not, it shall not perish.
Thou shalt see the pure: gardens are their abode:
And for the unbelievers is Hell-fire blazing:
And in life is disgrace, and that they should die:
That with which their breasts shall be oppressed shall they meet[1]."

[1] أربّاً واحداً ام الف رب   أدين اذا تقسمت الامور
عزلت اللات والعزّى جميعاً   كذلك يفعل الجلد الصبور

Throughout this whole account we notice that Ibn Hishâm is scrupulously careful to give us the very words which his predecessor Ibn Isḥâq had used in his narrative. We have therefore something definite to go upon in considering the history and beliefs of these reformers, and especially of Zaid, whose touching story and whose noble verses show what an influence for good he might have exercised upon Muḥammad. We shall see reason to believe that he did exercise[1] a certain amount of influence, and we may well wish it had had more effect upon Muḥammad's life and character.

Ibn Hishâm, again on Ibn Isḥâq's authority

فلا عزّى ادين ولا ابنتيها ولا صنميّ بني عمرو ازور
ولا غنماً ادين وكان ربّاً لنا في الدهر اذ حلمي يسير
عجبت وفي الليالي معجبات وفي الايام يعرفها البصير
بان الله قد افنى رجالاً كثيراً كان شأنهم الفجور
وابقى آخرين ببرّ قوم فيربل منهم الطفل الصغير
وبينا المرء يعثر ثاب يوماً كما يتروّح الغصن المطير
ولكن اعبد الرحمن ربي ليغفر ذنبي الرب الغفور
فتقوى الله ربكم احفظوها متى لا تحفظوها لا تبور
ترى الابرار دارهم جنان وللكفار حاميةٌ سعير
وخزيٌ في الحيوة وان يموتوا يلاقوا ما تضيق بهِ الصدور

Sîratu'r Rasûl, vol. i, p. 77.

[1] Imâm Abû'l Faraḥ in his *Kitâbu'l Aghânî* (pt. III, p. 15) tells us that Muḥammad had met and conversed with Zaid ibn 'Amr before the former received inspiration.

informs us that Al Khaṭṭâb, who was Zaid's uncle, reproved the latter for abandoning the religion of his people, and persecuted him to such an extent that he was unable to live in Mecca any longer. He seems to have travelled in other parts of the country, but at last took up his residence in a cave on Mount Ḥirâ [1]. There he lived to a great age, and when he died he was buried at the foot of the mountain. His death is said to have occurred only five years before Muḥammad first put forth, in A.D. 612, his claim to the prophetic office. Now Ibn Isḥâq tells us that it was the custom of the Quraish "in the Days of Ignorance" to leave the city and spend a month upon Mount Ḥirâ—the month of Ramaḍân, as he implies—every year in the practice of penance (*taḥannuth*) [2]. It is clear that it was in consequence of this custom that Muḥammad afterwards selected the whole of that particular month to be observed by his followers for ever as a time of abstinence. As it fell in summer in his time, this retreat may have been a welcome change to the wealthier members of the community, who were thus enabled to leave for a time the hot and close streets of an

[1] *Sîratu'r Rasûl*, vol. i, p. 79.

[2] ثم جاءه جبريل بما جاءه من كرامة الله وهو بحرآء في شهر رمضان . . . كان رسول الله يجاور في حرآء من كل سنة شهراً وكان ذلك مما تحنث به قريش في الجاهلية والتحنث التبرّر . . . قال ابن هشام تقول العرب التحنّث التحنّف يريدون الحنيفية فيبدلون الفاء من الثاء (*Op. cit.*, vol. i, pp. 80, 81.)

unhealthy Eastern city for the pure air of the open country. We have no reason to suppose that asceticism played any considerable part in their life at that period. Muḥammad, we are expressly told, used to observe this custom of spending the month of Ramaḍân every year at Mount Ḥirâ: and he was actually living in the very cave once inhabited by Zaid, when, as he believed, the first revelation came to him through the Angel Gabriel. It is an error to see in this any special "retirement from the world" on the part of Muḥammad on that occasion, since we are told that his wife Khadîjah was with him, and he was only following the custom [1] of his tribe.

It is evident that, during this yearly visit to Mount Ḥirâ, Muḥammad had every opportunity of conversing with Zaid. Muḥammad's reverence for the man is clearly shown by Tradition. We have already seen that he afterwards acknowledged that Zaid might be prayed for after his death: and this is the more noteworthy because Baiḍâwî, in his commentary upon Sûrah IX., At Taubah, 114, states that Muḥammad was forbidden to pray for the salvation of his own mother Âminah, to whom he was tenderly attached, and who had died in his early youth. Moreover, Al Wâqidî states that Muḥammad "gave Zaid the salutation of Peace, an honour vouchsafed only to Muslims, that he invoked God's grace on him and affirmed, 'I have seen Him in

[1] Vide the preceding note, which is of great importance.

Paradise: he is drawing a train after him.' Sprenger ... says, 'Muḥammad openly acknowledged Zaid as his precursor, and every word known as Zaid's we find again in the Qur'ân [1].'" For instance, in Sûrah III., Âl 'Imrân, 19, Muḥammad is bidden to say to the common people, "Have ye become Muslims?" or "Have ye surrendered to God?" These words are said by Ibn Isḥaq [2] to have been addressed to the people by Zaid in the first place. Everyone of the main principles which we have found mentioned as inculcated by Zaid is dwelt upon in the Qur'ân also. Among these may be instanced: (1) the prohibition of killing infant daughters by burying them alive, according to the cruel custom of the Arabs of the time; (2) the acknowledgment of the Unity of God; (3) the rejection of idolatry and the worship of Al-Lât, Al-'Uzza' and the other deities of the people; (4) the promise of future happiness in Paradise or the "Garden"; (5) the warning of the punishment reserved in hell for the wicked; (6) the denunciation of God's wrath upon the "Unbelievers"; and (7) the application of the titles *Ar Raḥmân* (the Merciful), *Ar Rabb* (the Lord), and *Al Ghafûr* (the Forgiving) to God. Moreover, Zaid and all the other reformers (*Ḥanîfs*) claimed to be searching for the "Religion of Abraham." Besides all this,

[1] Koelle, *Moḥammed and Moḥammedanism*, p. 53.

[2] Quoted by Sprenger, *Life of Muḥammad*, p. 42.

the Qur'ân repeatedly [1], though indirectly [2], speaks of Abraham as a *Hanîf*, the chosen title of Zaid and his friends.

The root from which this word *Hanîf* is derived means in Hebrew "to conceal, to pretend, to lie, to be a hypocrite," and in Syriac its meanings are similar. In Arabic it seems to have first denoted "limping," or "walking unevenly," but came to signify *impiety* in abandoning the worship of the popular deities. In this sense it was doubtless at first applied to the reformers as a reproach. But since, as Ibn Hishâm tells us [3], in the pronunciation of the Quraish the word denoting "penance" and "purity" was confounded with the term denoting "Hanîfism," it is probable that the *Hanîfs* gladly adopted the name as expressing their abjuration of idolatry with all its abominations. It is none the less remarkable, however, that Muhammad should have ventured to apply the term to Abraham, and to invite men to become Hanîfs by returning to the "Religion of Abraham," which he identified with Islâm as proclaimed by himself. In fact, by this use of the word, Muhammad in the clearest possible manner declared his adhesion to the doctrines of the reformers. When in addition to this we find him adopting their teaching and incor-

[1] *e. g.*, Sûrahs III., 89; IV., 124; VI., 162.

[2] Arabic scholars will see in what the indirectness consists. Perhaps there is no real reason to say 'indirectly,' the language is so nearly direct.

[3] Above, p. 269, note 2.

porating it into the Qur'ân, we cannot hesitate to recognize the dogmas of the Ḥanîfs as forming one of the main Sources of Islâm.

That the Ḥanîfs should have exercised such an influence upon nascent Islâm was very natural for family reasons also. All the four leading reformers at Mecca were related to Muḥammad, being descended from a common ancestor Liwa'. Moreover, 'Ubaidu'llâh was a son of a maternal aunt of Muḥammad, and the latter married this reformer's widow, as we have already seen. Two others, Waraqah and 'Uthmân, were cousins of his first wife Khadîjah, as we learn from the genealogies given by Ibn Hishâm[1].

One objection may possibly occur to the reader who has patiently followed us so far in our investigations into the origin of Islâm. He may perhaps say, "All this is very similar to the play of Hamlet with the part of the Prince of Denmark left out. You have shown that the whole of Islâm has been borrowed from previously existent systems, and have therefore left nothing which can properly be attributed to Muḥammad himself. Is it not strange to find Muḥammadanism without a Muḥammad?" The answer to this objection is not far to seek. The creed of Islâm, to-day as in the past, shows what a very important part Muḥammad plays in

[1] *Sîratu'r Rasûl*, pp. 63, 76, &c.

S

the religious system of Muslims, for it consists, as Gibbon has well said, of an eternal truth and a necessary fiction: "There is no God but God: Muḥammad is the Apostle of God." It is not too much to say that in the minds of his followers Muḥammad holds as important a place as Jesus Christ does in those of Christians. The influence of his example for good or ill affects the whole Muḥammadan world in even the smallest matters, and few men have played a more momentous part in the religious, moral, and political history of the human race than the founder of Islâm.

It was naturally impossible that, occupying the position which he claimed for himself, Muḥammad should not have left upon the religion which he founded the distinct impress of his own personality. A builder collects his materials from many different quarters, yet their method and arrangement reveal his skill. The plan of the architect is manifested in the edifice which has been erected as its embodiment. Just in the same way, though we have seen that Muḥammad borrowed ideas, legends, and religious rites from many different quarters, the religion of Islâm has assumed a form of its own, which differs in certain respects from any other faith with which it may be compared. The beauty of the literary style of many parts of the Qur'ân has been universally admired, and it evidences the eloquence of its author in no doubtful manner. Its want of arrangement and harmony of design may not be due to him, but the work as a whole mirrors forth the limitations of Muḥammad's intellect, the very slight amount of real knowledge and learning that he possessed, his unlimited credulity and want of all critical faculty, and the moral defects of his character. When studied in the chronological order of its composition, the Qur'ân shows traces of a gradual change of policy which corresponds with the alteration in Muḥammad's own position and prospects in temporal matters. Certain parts of it are, even by Muḥammadan commentators, explained by reference to important events in his life, to which the "revelation" of these particular verses was directly due. To demonstrate this it will be sufficient to inquire *firstly* into Muḥammad's attitude in reference to the use of the sword in the spread of Islâm, and *secondly* into but one incident in his matrimonial relations.

It is well known that, before he left Mecca and took refuge in Medina in A.D. 622, Muḥammad had no temporal power. His followers in Mecca itself amounted to only a few score [1], and therefore had on two occasions—in 615 and again in 616—to seek safety in flight to Abyssinia. Accordingly, in those verses and Sûrahs which were composed before the Hijrah, no mention

[1] The total number of those who went to Abyssinia on the occasion of the second migration was 101, of whom 83 were men. (Sir W. Muir's *Life of Mahomet*, p. 84.)

whatever is made of the duty of taking up arms for the spread of the faith, or even in self-defence. But after the Hijrah, when many of the people of Medina had become his "Helpers," he in the first place gave permission to his "Companions" to fight for the protection of their own lives. Ibn Hishâm[1] observes that this permission was for the first time given in these verses: "It is permitted to those who fight because they are treated wrongfully . . . those who have been expelled from their dwellings unjustly, merely because they say, 'Our Lord is God'" (Sûrah XXII., Al Hajj, 40, 41). After a time, when victory had attended Muḥammad's arms on several plundering expeditions directed against the caravans belonging to the Quraish, this permission was turned into a command. Accordingly we read in Sûrah II., Al Baqarah, 212, 214: "War is fated for you, although it is hateful to you. . . . They ask thee concerning the month in which war is prohibited. Say thou: 'War in it is a serious matter, and so is hindering from the way of God, and unbelief in Him and in the Sacred Mosque; and the expulsion of His people from it is more serious in God's sight, and rebellion is worse than slaughter.'" This means that the Muslims were bidden to fight, even during the time when war was forbidden by the unwritten law of the Arabs, and not permit their enemies to

[1] *Sîratu'r Rasûl*, vol. i, p. 164, on the authority of 'Urwah and others.

hinder them from having access to the Ka'bah. Thirdly, when, in the sixth year of the Hijrah, the Muslims had overcome the Banû Quraidhah and certain other Jewish tribes, the command to engage in the Holy War, or *Jihâd*, became still sterner; for in Sûrah V., Al Mâidah, 37, it is written: "Verily the punishment of those who fight against God and His Apostle and strive to do evil in the land is that they be slain, or be crucified, or have their hands and their feet cut off on opposite sides, or be expelled from the land: that is a punishment for them in the world, and for them in the next life is reserved great torment." It may be observed that the Commentators explain that this decree refers to the treatment to be inflicted on idolaters, not on Jews and Christians. But the conduct which Muslims should observe towards the "People of the Book" was prescribed some years later, shortly before Muḥammad's death, in the eleventh year of the Hijrah. Then the fourth stage is reached in Sûrah IX., At Taubah, 5 and 29—probably the latest in date of all the Sûrahs of the Qur'ân—where it is commanded that, after the conclusion of the four Sacred Months of that year, the Muslims should recommence the war. The command in these verses runs thus: "Accordingly when the Sacred Months are past, then slay the Polytheists wherever ye find them, and take them and besiege them and lay wait for them with every ambuscade. If therefore they repent and raise the prayers and bring the alms[1], then free them on their way: verily God is forgiving, merciful. . . . Fight with those of them who have been brought the Book, who believe not in God nor in the Last Day, and who forbid not what God and His Apostle have forbidden, and who hold not the true religion, until they give the tribute[2] out of hand and be humbled." Thus the law of God as revealed in the Qur'ân was modified in proportion to the success of Muḥammad's arms. To account for this it was laid down as a rule that certain verses were superseded and annulled by others revealed later, according to what is said in Sûrah II., Al Baqarah, 100: "As for what We abrogate of a verse or cause thee to forget it, We bring a better than it or one like it: knowest thou not that God is able to do everything?" From that time to this, however, Muḥammadan jurists have not been able to decide which verses have been annulled and which others have taken their place, though some 225 are supposed to have been thus abrogated.

We might in the same way trace the change in Muḥammad's attitude towards Jews and Christians from the beginning of his career, when he hoped to win them over to his side, to the time when, finding himself disappointed in this expectation, he resolved to turn upon them with the sword. But

[1] That is, the alms prescribed for *Muslims* to give: *i.e.* become Muslims.

[2] The *jizyah*-tax, imposed on Jews and Christians.

we learn the same lesson from all such investigations, and that is how completely Muḥammad adapted his pretended revelations to what he believed to be the need of the moment.

The same thing is true with regard to what we read in Sûrah Al Aḥzâb regarding the circumstances attending his marriage with Zainab, whom his adopted son Zaid divorced for his sake. The subject is too unsavoury for us to deal with at any length, but a reference to what the Qur'ân itself (Sûrah XXXIII., 37) says about the matter, coupled with the explanations afforded by the Commentators and the Traditions, will prove that Muḥammad's own character and disposition have left their mark upon the moral law of Islâm and upon the Qur'ân itself. The licence given to him, and to him alone, in the Qur'ân to marry[1] more than the legal number of four wives at a time allowed to each Muslim is an additional proof to the same effect, and it is explained by a very unpleasant Tradition which contains a saying of 'Âyishah in reference to his idiosyncrasies.

All this being considered, it is clear that, although Muḥammad borrowed religious practices, beliefs, and legends from various different sources, yet he combined them in some measure into one more or less consistent whole, thus producing the religion of Islâm. Some parts of this are good, and Islâm contains certain great truths, borrowed from other

[1] Surah XXXIII., Al Aḥzâb, 49.

systems of religion, which in a measure account for its continued existence in the world. But it certainly does not contain a single new or lofty religious conception, and its general tone is all too faithful a reflexion of the carnal and sensual nature of its founder. To use an Oriental simile is not perhaps inappropriate in speaking of such a thoroughly local and Oriental religion as Muḥammadanism. Islam therefore may aptly be compared with:

> "That bituminous lake where Sodom flamed,"

which, receiving into its bosom the waters of many streams that, thus united, assume the shape and form of its basin, turns them all into one great widespread Sea of Death, from whose shores rise pestilential exhalations destructive to all life within reach of their malign influence. Such is Islâm. Originating from many different sources and receiving into it certain elements of truth, it has assumed its form from the character and disposition of Muḥammad; and thus the good in it serves only to recommend and preserve the evil which renders it a false and delusive faith, a curse to men and not a blessing—one that has turned into deserts many of the fairest regions of the earth, that has, even in our own days, deluged many a land with innocent blood, and has smitten with a moral, intellectual, and spiritual blight every nation of men which lies under its iron yoke and groans beneath its pitiless sway.

INDEX

[The numbers refer to the pages.]